Investigating Troublesome Classroom Behaviour

This book is intended for early years and primary school teachers who want to spend more time helping children learn and less time dealing with persistent misbehaviour. Drawing on the experience of teaches and children, it describes how teachers can investigate troublesome behaviours in order to plan interventions that are right for the child, the teacher and the context. In this book, the author:

- Explains how evidence-based practice can help promote social justice in schools.
- Outlines basic research skills to help teachers begin investigating their own practice.
- Offers practical suggestions for developing positive learning relationships.
- Encourages teachers to work together and to adapt ideas to their own classroom environment.

Illustrated with useful case studies, anecdotes and questions, this is a practical and down-to-earth book that will help teachers of young children make lasting changes in their classrooms.

Loraine Corrie is Co-Director of the Centre for Early Childhood Research and Development at the Hong Kong Institute of Education.

Investigating Troublesome Classroom Behaviour

Practical tools for teachers

Loraine Corrie

RoutledgeFalmer
Taylor & Francis Group
London and New York

First published 2002
by RoutledgeFalmer
11 New Fetter Lane, London EC4P 4EE

Simultaneously published in the USA and Canada
by RoutledgeFalmer
29 West 35th Street, New York, NY 10001

RoutledgeFalmer is an imprint of the Taylor & Francis Group

Typeset in Sabon by
HWA Text and Data Management Ltd
Printed and bound in Great Britain by
The Cromwell Press, Trowbridge, Wiltshire

British Library Cataloguing in Publication Data
A catalogue record for this book is available from the British Library

Library of Congress Cataloging in Publication Data
Corrie, Loraine
Investigating troublesome classroom behaviour
Loraine Corrie
p. cm.
Includes bibliographic references and index
1. Classroom management. 2. Behavior modification. I. Title

LB 3013.C567 2002
37.102´4–dc21 2001041827

ISBN 0-415-23709-2 (hbk)
ISBN 0-415-23710-6 (pbk)

To Michael and James Corrie – my sons, my teachers

'Not knowing how near the Truth is
We seek it far away – what a pity! …'
Hakiun (1760) Song of Zazen

Contents

Figures

Acknowledgements

The author and publisher wish to express their gratitude to the following: Linda Gerovich for permission to reproduce material from her unpublished research project 'Seven-year-old attention-deficit/hyperactivity disordered boys in primary school settings'; Lisa Moore for permission to reproduce material from her thesis 'Teachers' knowledge and practice of empowering young children in four early childhood settings in Australia and the United Kingdom'; The Australian Early Childhood Association for permission to reproduce material from Loraine Corrie and Natalie Leitao, 'Young children's knowledge of their support networks and social competence' *Australian Journal of Early Childhood*, 24(3), 25–31; Taylor and Francis Ltd, 11 New Fetter Lane, London EC4P 4EE, for permission to reproduce a modified version of Loraine Corrie, 'Facilitating newly qualified teachers' growth as collaborative practitioners', *Asia-Pacific Journal of Education* 28(2), 111–21; New Zealand Early Childhood Research Network for permission to reproduce material from Loraine Corrie ' Contributing to educational change as a teacher–researcher', *New Zealand Research in Early Childhood Education*, 2, 29–40; National Foundation for Educational Research in England and Wales for permission to reproduce material from Loraine Corrie, 'Managing troublesome classroom behaviour at group time' *Topics*, 22, 1–7. All unattributed quotations are from unpublished research for my PhD thesis 'Pedagogical knowledge and classroom practice: teachers' management of a disruptive classroom behaviour, Talking out of Turn' University of London, Institute of Education.

Introduction

I have written this book for practitioners and intending practitioners who want to know more about children's classroom behaviour. One theme running through the book is that creating productive learning communities best begin by investigating the context of children's behaviours in systematic ways. Change is likely to be effective when teachers use valid information as the starting point for their plans and actions. Another theme is that fostering learning relationships in schools is one of the most critical aspects of teaching.

You will find that theory is woven with practice throughout the book and illustrated with stories about classroom life. Some readers will want to know more about certain topics and theories, and for this reason I have added references for you to consult. These references will provide you with more details about the theoretical base of the book.

This book draws on research that I conducted in inner London that investigated how teachers managed classroom behaviour, as well as other studies in the United Kingdom and Australia. In addition, I refer to the work of many researchers from different contexts from the United States of America and the United Kingdom, to Australia, Canada, New Zealand and the Asia-Pacific region.

The book is informed by my practical experience as an early childhood and primary school teacher in Australia and the United Kingdom. My teaching experience includes working with 5 to 13-year-old children who were withdrawn from schools because of their challenging behaviours. These children caused chaos in their classrooms, and many were aggressive and manipulative until they experienced trust relationships with staff. The children needed relationships that were based on consistency and they tested the limits vigorously. In this setting I learned the value of effective behaviour programmes and contexts that enabled children to build on their competencies and strengths.

I taught children in inner London who were newly arrived from war zones and vulnerable children living in poverty. Some of these children were silent, passive and compliant. It was hard to get to know them as it seemed that they would prefer the ground to swallow them up rather than attract the teacher's or peers' attention. They tended to withdraw from relationships and act as if they had no right to be in the class. Consequently, they had trouble learning because they were afraid to interact with others or to ask for help from either their peers or adults. They were tender flowers, frequently uprooted and moved to other schools before relationships could blossom, leaving staff to wonder how these children fared in the rough and tumble life of busy classrooms.

I worked with families from comfortable middle-class homes, where some parents visited my classroom regularly to check on their children's progress. Some of these parents were anxious about their children's progress and could be described as intrusive in their parenting style. Acting in the child's best interest as they saw it, they tended to want to control and organise every aspect of the child's life. The children depended on adults to tell them what to do, which meant they had difficulty in exploring, creating, innovating and problem solving, and this, in turn, impeded their growth of competency and self-confidence.

In recent years I have taught pre-service and in-service teacher education courses, and have conducted research with teachers at different stages of their careers. My work with teachers has taught me a great deal about relationships from the teachers' perspectives, including relationships with staff members and those in the management hierarchy in schools. Collegial relationships exert powerful influences on practitioners and facilitate professional growth, which is seen in many different aspects of practice.

Organisation of the book

Chapter 1 discusses the behaviours that concern teachers in today's classrooms. Typical problems are discussed and the stories of two teachers are used to illustrate the key points. The theoretical basis of the book is outlined.

Chapter 2 places the focus on learning relationships that help all children behave appropriately. Learning and behaving are seen as integrated components. The chapter discusses problems that emerge when teachers want children to use active learning for academic content but expect them to behave as if they were in traditional classrooms.

Chapter 3 focuses on the teacher as a key figure in the learning context. The chapter helps readers to understand more about their own theories of children's behaviour in order to help them construct some lasting change. The cases of three teachers are discussed to show that what they know about children's behaviour makes a different to their practice.

In Chapter 4 the system model is applied to classrooms to help readers understand how conditions of social justice may be eroded for some children in school. The cases of three children are used to look closely at the classroom, their relationships and their experiences. The cases are used to introduce you to a research method that you could use in your own classrooms.

Chapter 5 continues to think about children's behaviour in relation to school practices. Stories of newly-qualified teachers are used to explore ideas of social justice in schools, and to think about the difficulties of working alone as autonomous professionals. It is suggested that developing collaborative staff relationships is a key to making a difference to children's troublesome behaviour, and that the principal has a pivotal role in facilitating collaboration.

Chapter 6 asks teachers to rethink their teaching roles to include the 'teacher-researcher'. The chapter explores teachers' resistance to research by reporting a case study of one teacher who changed many of her ideas after having experience in classroom-based action research. The chapter explains how teachers' research can help them with troublesome classroom behaviour and it provides teachers with some tools to help them explore their classroom systems. In addition, the chapter introduces teachers to a technique known as the 'appreciative inquiry'. This research technique can identify what works in your classroom and what you do well so that you can have more of it. You can find out what the children like about your classroom, how they view their own strengths, and their hopes and dreams for school. The appreciative inquiry method builds on the positives and can strengthen trust relationships in classrooms. The method can be extended to include the whole school; school community, including parents and families, and the broader community.

Chapter 7 explains how to apply the skills of research to investigate a common troublesome behaviour, 'talking out of turn'. The chapter guides teachers to consider the classroom as a system with many interrelated components that may impact on the child's behaviour.

Chapter 8 concludes by reviewing the key elements of the book and stressing the need for socially just and ethical schools. Investigating the context of children's behaviour can lead to evidence-based practice, which may provide the best opportunities for children to achieve their academic and social potentials.

Chapter 1

What is troublesome behaviour?

This book is for teachers who want to spend more time helping children learn and less time dealing with troublesome behaviours. Most teachers want to create supportive classrooms where children achieve their potentials but this may be difficult to achieve. At times, children's behaviours disrupt teaching and learning and fill classrooms with tension.

Teachers find it hard to stay enthusiastic when they spend precious time managing children's behaviour. They feel frustrated when, despite their best efforts, nothing seems to change. This book takes the stance that teachers can achieve their goal of creating high quality learning communities but there are no easy answers.

No fairy godmother can wave a magic wand for you, and no behaviour management guru can give you a charismatic personality to make children putty in your hands forever. This book doesn't promise 'ten top tips' or lists of quick fixes. I hope it will help you to see some choices and some ways forward but you will have to work hard to create the classrooms of your dreams.

I aim to help you create ethical approaches that:

- are right for the sort of *teacher* you are;
- help the *children* you teach;
- fit with the *school's ethos and its leadership;*
- match the values of the children's *families*;
- suit the *education system* that employs you.

You will make the best sense of this book if you talk about the issues raised with a teaching colleague, or alternatively, have a conversation through note making. Many teachers find that keeping professional journals and recording their thoughts and responses helps them clarify their understandings and the issues they need to think through. Try to relate the material you are reading to your own experience, context, and what you know and value.

Teachers have made lasting change in their classrooms by thinking seriously about what they know about teaching, why they do what they do in classrooms, and by talking with teaching colleagues. I aim to help you to identify the ways that *you* think about children's behaviour, and the ways in which the school thinks about it. In addition, I will suggest strategies to investigate your classrooms in order to help children learn new ways of behaving.

Investigating behaviour in your classroom

Children's troublesome behaviours show no sign of decreasing. Why? Some people claim that teachers don't have the skills that they need to manage classrooms effectively. However, many educators don't agree that helping children to behave appropriately is just about using certain skills or strategies. It seems that teaching has become more complex than ever before with layers of difficulty being added to the job. Teachers bring enormous expertise to the classroom, but changes to society and education require them to add new understandings about children's troublesome behaviour.

Complex situations mean that simple solutions will not result in lasting change and will not help teachers and children to enjoy their lives at school. As you read this book I hope you will understand how you can become a researcher in your own classroom so that you can investigate the behaviours that you find troublesome. Try not to be put off by the word 'researcher' and the mystic that tends to surround it, as many of the skills are second nature to teachers. I think you'd agree that many teachers use research skills as they:

- gather accurate information about children's academic progress;
- use the information to plan and implement change.

Being a researcher means inquiring into a problem in a systematic way so that staff can take different perspectives of the situation. Investigating classrooms and schools helps teachers design interventions that are based on evidence rather than an individual's hunch or gut feelings.

Evidence-based practice

Investigating troublesome behaviours can help teachers to plan and implement evidence-based practice that makes a positive difference to classroom life. Schools can foster good learning relationships when they gather objective evidence upon which to plan and implement change.

The term 'evidence-based practice' has been used mainly in the medical field. Medical experts have assumed that procedures used in medicine, such as the lengthy 'scrub-up' before operations, were derived from scientific research. However, recently doctors have found that there was little research to support many procedures and they are now calling for evidence-based medicine.

Similar issues apply in education when practices may become established without good research support. At times, research findings conducted in one context are applied to a different context, but they may not be appropriate. At times, new research shows that old ways of doing things did not work but schools continue on with the familiar practice. When teachers and schools investigate troublesome behaviour they can ensure that the findings are relevant to the children, classrooms and schools where they teach, this will help them design effective change.

Evidence-based practice enables practitioners to develop greater professionalism that comes from being informed, which helps to build confidence. Teachers who are researchers:

- identify issues;
- investigate questions;
- try out new strategies;
- monitor their effectiveness in ways that are relevant to their schools;
- change the interventions if necessary;
- monitor the changes;
- share their experiences with others.

Many teachers find it better to get together with other people to research an issue. Teachers who collaborate with their colleagues understand how much two or more people can achieve by sharing their knowledge and skills.

This book invites you to think deeply about issues that concern you, reflect on what you know, do, value and believe in, and then to construct some new ways of thinking and doing that are right for you and the classrooms where you spend your days.

Teachers' work

Working with children brings teachers a great deal of joy. Teachers know they are important people in children's lives, and stories shared in staff rooms reveal how much teachers value the fact that their work makes a real contribution to children's learning and growth.

Yet the downside of teaching is managing the relentless grind of nitty-gritty behaviour that disrupts teaching and learning (Elton, 1989). It is the sheer number of times that teachers have to repeat themselves that wears them out: 'Get on with your work!' 'Stop talking!' and 'Please pay attention'. The majority of troublesome classroom behaviours are the low-level kind rather than major acts of defiance, aggression or delinquency (Fields, 1986; Tulley and Chiu, 1998; Wheldall and Merrett, 1988).

Teachers say the following types of behaviours cause them concern:

- needing constant supervision;
- not listening to directions;

- often playing with pens, pencils, and other items;
- slow getting started – needing to be 'pushed' to begin work;
- talking out of turn, whispering, giggling, laughing;
- being unmotivated;
- getting distracted from work easily;
- often seeking attention

(Fields, 1986, p. 51)

The media would have us believe that teachers worry more about serious acts of violence than other sorts of challenging behaviour. Aggression appears to be on the rise (Malone, Bonitz and Rickett, 1998), but most teachers report that major acts of violence happen rarely in their primary school classrooms or early childhood settings.

Do you find some types of behaviour cause you concern in the classroom? If so, try and specify the behaviour.

Does this behaviour disrupt your teaching?

Does this behaviour disrupt children's learning?

Do you find this behaviour annoying? If you do, then explain how.

You may find it interesting to ask some of your teaching colleagues about the behaviours that concern them, as their answers may help you identify common causes of concern.

Teachers find that managing frequent disruptive behaviours every day erodes teaching and learning time in their classrooms, which leaves them feeling frustrated. Dealing with annoying behaviours over and over again increases teachers' dissatisfaction with their work.

It is the nitty-gritty behaviours that are the focus of this book rather than the behaviours exhibited by children with clinical conditions or diagnosed special needs. Although Chapter 4 reports three cases of children with attention deficit hyperactivity disorder, you will see that their behaviours tend not to be major acts of rebellion, aggression or defiance.

Some teachers worry about their capacity to deal with the range of psychological and sociological problems that children bring to school, and feel they are being pushed into the roles of counsellors or social workers without proper training. Teachers find that their additional pastoral roles erode time for teaching and many feel that this is not part of their work, but is it time to redefine teachers' work? Many teachers are surprised when they analyse their working week to find that their traditional ideas of teaching have to be broadened to include other elements that are central to their role as teacher. The following questions ask you to think about the work that makes up your week.

Take some time to think about a typical teaching week. List all your activities and responsibilities.

Look at your list.

How many of the duties involve working directly with children, either whole class, small group or 1:1? What percentage of your teaching duties involves a wide range of organising, managing and care responsibilities that do not include direct teaching?

I am sure your list shows that your professional life is filled with many duties other than helping children learn knowledge, skills and positive attitudes. No doubt your list of duties includes a whole raft of managing and organising responsibilities such as:

- creating a practical and attractive physical environment;
- gathering and organising materials, equipment and tools for learning;
- creating a supportive and encouraging psychological environment for learning;
- assessing children's learning outcomes in order to plan appropriate curriculum;
- planning for children's personal and social development, together with academic skills;
- organising school events, such as assemblies or sports' day;
- organising excursions and incursions;
- collecting money for special events;
- meeting with parents, other professionals, staff and the principal;
- documenting children's progress and reporting to parents, principals and other professionals.

Ideas of traditional teaching work have to be expanded to fit the diverse roles that teachers enact each week. In addition to the duties listed above, teachers have to keep up-to-date with innovations and educational change mandated by the system that employs them. Many teachers have had to grapple with changes associated with outcomes-based education that include system-level curriculum reform, assessment and evaluation of children's progress to learning outcomes and performance indicators for teachers. In addition, changes to society and family life mean that teachers may have to deal with children in crises and this means being equipped and confident to manage a range of difficult situations (Hardin and Harris, 2000).

Managing change

The broad scope of system-level innovations and the fast pace of change may leave teachers feeling stretched to their limit, and dealing with troublesome behaviours on top of everything else may be a breaking point. A wide range of duties, together with responding to children going through hard times, place a great deal of strain on teachers as they juggle tasks throughout the day. Time is a commodity that teachers value highly and knowing how to use time properly is important to their survival in schools.

The teachers I know abhor wasting time and have learnt how to deal with diverse demands in rapid succession to save time. When they experience difficulties managing children's behaviour, they don't want to go into in-depth analysis and yearn for some straightforward solutions from an expert that will work. Yet, again and again, they are disappointed with the advice that they receive from outsiders because it never seems to be quite right for their situation.

Teachers find quick-fix solutions don't work, but continue to search out new discipline techniques. They are filled with hope when the new techniques seem to make a difference for a while, only to be disappointed when the novelty effects fade and children's troublesome behaviours return as strongly as ever.

Teachers need to add to their teaching repertoires by trying out new ideas, but it is unrealistic to hope that simple solutions will make a difference to difficult problems. Teachers know that their work is complex and there is plenty of research evidence to support their view. However, teaching is often talked about as if it's easy, which demeans the profession and undermines teachers' confidence and self-esteem. As the following section illustrates, a close look at any classroom at any time of the school day shows that teaching is fast-paced, multi-faceted and intellectually demanding activity.

Looking in the classroom

Go into any primary or early childhood classroom and what do you see? The classroom is a dynamic humming environment, full of relationships that are shaped and reshaped through a myriad of interactions. The interactions can be fleeting and hard to spot: a quick twitch of an eyebrow, a pencil moved slightly to the right, or a whispered 'Get lost'. In the process of interaction, feelings are hurt, irritation flares, and revenge is promised, or friendship blossoms as smiles are shared. Children signal messages to their friends (and enemies) and teachers use a smile, a frown, a single word or phrase to convey a whole range of meanings that are built up within the group over time.

The following snapshot of a classroom highlights the relationship dynamics that shape the actions of children and teachers:

> The teacher sighed and signalled to the boys to put the gum in the bin. As they pushed their chairs noisily on the floor, a muffled giggle from Sharon's table caught the teacher's attention: 'If you girls can't read quietly I'm going to have to separate you. I've told you already and I won't tell you again'. A little later the girls' whispering and giggling means they are moved.

> They changed places noisily with cross looks and indignant, 'It's not fair', and, 'I didn't say a thing'. The brief after-lunch calm in the room changed and the time for quiet reading was over.

The teacher, Maria, talked about her difficulties later at a support group. She related how the children's behaviour had led her to decide not to do the science lesson on flight that afternoon because she thought the children wouldn't be able to handle being all over the room making things. So she got out some worksheets and played videotapes they enjoyed the previous week. You may have noticed that the behaviour that concerned Maria was not major acts of aggression or disruption. It was the ongoing nitty-gritty behaviour (such as *not following the teacher's instructions properly* and *talking out of turn*) that led her to change her teaching plans for the afternoon.

As she talked she became clear about the confusions she felt about the gap between the way she wanted to teach and the actions she found herself taking. Like many teachers, Maria had good days when the children were responsive and teaching was a breeze. The good days gave her a real buzz and filled her with hope, but they didn't come often enough. Too many days were filled with repeating instructions, giving warnings, sorting out skirmishes, and managing uncompliant behaviour.

Maria felt pessimistic about her potential to change the classroom dynamics but seemed surprised when she was asked where she went for help. She told the group that everybody in her school was too busy and she couldn't trouble them. She added that as a qualified teacher she should be able to cope with her problems.

The other teachers responded to Maria with sympathetic nods, and shared similar frustrations about feeling more like police officers engaged in crowd control rather than helping children learn. You may be able to relate to these teachers. They knew that their behaviour management strategies were not working and they wanted to do things differently. Like many caring and dedicated professionals, these teachers understood it was time to take stock of classrooms and how they responded to children's troublesome behaviour.

Managing behaviour or managing classrooms?

Teachers have to deal with the behaviour that disrupts teaching and learning in order to create and maintain high-quality learning environments, but many teachers struggle to achieve this goal. It's been said that teachers have difficulties because they lack the skills needed to manage their classrooms effectively (Elton, 1989). However, the skills are not complex and countless lists of 'hints for good classroom management' urge teachers to:

- establish and maintain a set of few rules;
- establish clear consequences for acts of inappropriate and appropriate behaviour;

- give clear instructions;
- be prepared and well organised;
- plan appropriate learning experiences.

Teachers know about these valuable skills, which have been researched and promoted in education for many years. You might want to return to the seminal work of authors such as Kounin (1971) and Gordon (1974) to remind yourself of the key principles of classroom management that no teacher can afford to ignore.

Many teachers are knowledgeable about the principles of classroom management and want to implement them, but something happens between the knowing and doing. One reason why the management skills are complex is that teaching is rarely about cause and effect: it's about relationships. There is nothing new in the idea that relationships are central to learning, for example see Ginott's (1972) classic work, but the emphasis on behaviourism in the 1980s tended to lead educators away from this aspect of classrooms.

Let's think about learning relationships and what happens when a teacher gives an instruction to the class, for example, 'Clear your desks ready for music'. Teachers don't just give clear instructions to thin air or to thirty compliant responders. Teachers give an instruction to students who receive it, interpret it, and decide on a course of action. Of course, there are no guarantees that the students will decide to behave in the way the teacher wants. For example, when a teacher gives an instruction he/she might expect that some children will:

- comply at once;
- comply slowly … in their own time;
- comply just a little;
- appear not to have heard, so the teacher has to repeat the instruction;
- do something else.

What happens when you give instructions to the whole class?

Monitor this for a morning – keep a record of children's responses:

Give an instruction and then notice:

How many children respond quickly?

How many children respond slowly?

How many appear not to have heard?

How many do something different?

How often do you repeat instructions?

Do children's responses vary according to the type of instruction you've given?

Try it out: something you know the children aren't keen on: 'Get your pads out for a spelling test' and something you know the children like: 'Clear your tables for playtime'.

Think of a time when children responded quickly and easily.

What were the elements that made that time a success?

How can you have more of it?

Mike's room may sound familiar to you. As you read the story try to think about the complexity of classroom relationships that you experience and how they shape your moment-by-moment decisions.

> Mike (in his first year of teaching) instructed children to return to their desk from the carpet and get certain materials they needed for maths activities at the learning stations. Mike directed the children to gather their materials and wait for the next instruction:
>
> Ten children immediately went to their desks and took out the materials they needed for maths. Approximately eight children dispersed to various parts of the room, where two seemed to be looking for a pencil sharpener, two were chatting to other children, and two were taking circular routes back to their seats. Two children continued to sit on the carpet and made no attempt to move. One child stared into space and the other one jumped up and called the teacher's name in a loud voice, saying he'd just remembered he didn't put his lunch order in.
>
> Mike said he had several thoughts running through his head as he noticed who had and had not carried out his instruction. He made his way to the front of the class and repeated his instruction for children to sit in their seats and get ready for maths. He knew he had to gather up the stragglers, sort out the problems and engage the class as quickly as possible. At least three minutes had passed since the first instruction, and Mike saw that some waiting children are fidgety, but that some children were not seated. He repeated his original instruction again for the third time, and a tide of anger washed over him. Without thinking he slammed a book onto his desk and yelled, 'Sit down now you morons!' Suddenly all the children in the room were seated, silent and staring at him with frightened eyes.

Using aggressive strategies, like yelling and name-calling, was not in Mike's list of desirable teaching skills and he regretted it as soon as it happened. He knew that he was presenting a poor role model to the children and that scaring children into submission was never going to solve management problems. He knew that he couldn't develop good working relationships with children if he bullied them or failed to treat them with respect (Johns, 2000).

Why did Mike lose self-control? There had been layer upon layer of interruptions to teaching and learning that finally got too much for him for a split second. Many teachers will empathise with Mike and recognise the dynamics that mark teacher–children relationships. Like all teachers, Mike's relationships with the children in his class have histories and are built up over time. Mike's frustration wasn't just about getting ready for maths or the fact that some children didn't follow his instructions that particular time. It was an accumulation of slow-downs, interruptions and delays to teaching and learning over the past weeks.

At week six of the school year Mike knew the class and he anticipated which children he could rely on to follow the classroom routines and who would subvert the process at every step. He found himself beginning to tighten up in the stomach when he looked around the room and saw the same few children doing the wrong thing.

The children influenced Mike's behaviour as much as he influenced their behaviour, but later, when Mike thought about the day, it was hard for him to see all the elements that shaped the events. It was easy for Mike to see certain children as trouble-makers, but harder for him to see the two-way flow of interactions or the way that dynamics emerged.

Like many teachers, Mike was critical of his skills. He realised teachers cannot promote positive classroom behaviour when they have tantrums, use insults or berate children (Hardin and Harris, 2000). Mike knew that he needed to be a good role model who treats children with respect, but he didn't know what to do about his classroom management problems. There was nobody on the school staff he could talk to about his difficulties and he didn't want other people to know about them anyway. Mike said that the rest of the staff were experienced teachers and seemed to be doing a good job.

Mike decided that the troublesome behaviours meant he needed to improve his grip on the class by being firmer and making sure the children knew who was boss. He reasoned, 'It's just this sort of class. You've got to be tough with these kids'. Also, he thought he might have to drop the idea of activity-based learning centres and keep the children in their seats more. Had Mike cracked the code of classroom management? If you don't think so, then I wonder what advice you would give him if you were a teaching colleague. Aspects of classroom management that may provoke troublesome behaviour include irrelevant curriculum, poor instructional strategies and rigid classroom demands (Hardin and Harris, 2000). Teachers who yell, name call, threaten, or use sarcasm and social ridicule are using hostile means to control students that destroy trust relationships and increase stress for all (Johns, 2000).

Teachers may rely on strategies such as 'time out' or detention, but they are likely to find that these punitive measures do little to promote positive classrooms and appropriate behaviour, and neither do over-use of rewards (Kohn, 1993; Tulley and Chiu, 1998).

There are many strategies that teachers use to ensure that their classrooms run smoothly and they are central to an effective teacher's repertoire. Teachers know that *careful planning* is an essential part of teaching. Maria knew she was unlikely to have a really good day when she arrived late and unprepared for a class of energetic eight-year-olds. Nobody needs to tell Maria that *preparing and organising* are key classroom management skills that expert teachers make look so easy, and that designing *appropriate and motivating curriculum* is essential. All teachers need to spend a decent chunk of time getting themselves and their materials ready, and making sure that the learning experiences are appropriate and motivating.

Maria would be the first person to admit that planning and preparation were only part of the story, and that *consistency in applying rules* is essential to smooth-running classrooms. When she had time to think about it, Maria knew that she was giving children too many warnings and waiting too long before acting to stop uncompliant behaviour. She knew that she wouldn't gain children's trust when she gave them repeated warnings or tried to nag them into being compliant, rather than applying logical consequences swiftly.

Maria knew all the hints on the good management list, but said that nothing is as straightforward as the books make out. Maria gave warnings because she saw the children as 'good kids at heart', who get carried away sometimes. Maria said that she wanted to give the children a second chance because she knew some have a hard time at home.

Similarly, Mike understood the principles of behavioural approaches and knew that strategies used inconsistently will reinforce behaviours. However, he said that he found himself doing things he didn't want to do, and actually reinforcing the behaviour that was disrupting the classroom. Like many teachers, Mike knew he used ineffective strategies but as time went by he seemed to get locked into them (Malone, Bonitz and Rickett, 1998).

An outsider might find it strange that teachers actually do things that result in more troublesome behaviour, but outsiders don't usually understand the full range of dynamics that make classrooms complex places. Think about the following example:

> Mike decided to have the class together as a group for a discussion about the ocean, which was a topic that the class were beginning to study. Mike knew that managing discussions was hard and children tended to call out, take other children's turns to speak or interrupt him as he was explaining a key point. Mike remembered the classroom management strategy of restating the rules, and so he reminded the group about the 'hands up to speak' rule and explained why it is important. Mike ignored children who called out and made sure he gave their turn to another

student. Then he asked children to think of questions they'd like to investigate about the sea and Jarrad, a child usually reluctant to participate at group time, called out 'Why is the ocean salty?' and Mike responded, 'Great question, Jarrad', and wrote it on the board.

What behaviour did Mike reinforce?

How could he have more of the behaviour he wants at group time?

Think about your own classroom situation.

Is it possible that your behaviour reinforces children's inappropriate behaviour at times?

It may help you to think through a specific example and the dynamics that lead to it.

Later, Mike said he knew that there were times when he asked children to put their hands up for a turn to speak, then responded when they call out. He felt frustrated about the difficulties in managing talk, and understood how his response led to more calling out behaviour. Mike explained that everything happened very quickly:

> I told them to put their hands up and then somebody called out a great answer and it's Jarrad, who hardly ever contributes. I want to encourage him to be part of the group because the kids leave him out all the time. So, with all this running through my mind, I accepted his call out, and then other children called out their questions and soon everything was chaotic and I had to clamp down on them again.

Mike didn't need anybody to explain to him he transgressed principles central to the behavioural approach by intermittently reinforcing the children's calling-out behaviour. However, Mike was trying to balance what he knew about Jarrad's position in the classroom group with what he knows about guiding children's behaviour. Mike understood what was happening in his classroom, but found it hard to change because the relationship dynamics were more compelling than narrow classroom management principles.

Maria and Mike know about good classroom management strategies, but struggle to use them in their classrooms particularly when they are managing behaviour. There are many aspects of classroom management that teachers find quite easy to implement, such as:

- organising the physical environment;
- rearranging the furniture and physical environment;
- making decisions about timetables and classroom routines;
- defining rules that govern behaviour;

- planning a well-balanced, motivating and appropriate curriculum that meets the needs of a range of learners.

Management skills make a difference to children's behaviour but when we talk about managing children's behaviour it implies that there is a one-way flow of influence from teacher to child. As we saw with Mike, this simple view of classrooms bears little relation to the facts. In every verbal and non-verbal interaction that passes from teacher to student, or from one peer to another, the participants are engaged in a dance. The dance may result in perfect synchrony or it may result in treading on toes, but it evolves as a result of a two-way process between the participants.

Teachers and children engage in interactions that contribute to their relationships and in doing so they may:

- exchange ideas based on what they know;
- create ways of thinking about events, situations, problems and achievements;
- communicate feelings and wishes;
- form intentions and expectations;
- use histories to make predictions;
- shape values.

Actions, reactions, responses and initiatives emerge from interactions that may seem insignificant and unimportant. For example, a child turns away when her teacher asks a question. The teacher makes no comment and continues on to another child, but that fleeting interchange will contribute to the emerging teacher–child relationship.

Many teachers feel that they need to take action to deal with troublesome behaviour, but are wise enough to know that they need a sound basis for change to their practice. The following section presents the theoretical framework that can help you look again at children's behaviour in order to make positive and long-lasting changes.

The context of behaviour

Two important strands of research inform understandings about children's troublesome classroom behaviour. First, behaviour cannot be separated from the context in which it occurs, which means that children may behave in one way at school and another way at home and the difference may be supported by the context (Watkins and Wagner, 2000). Second, teachers make a great deal of difference to some children's long-term outcomes. Teachers do not have the power to change children's home backgrounds or family life, but research shows that teachers can guide children to developmental pathways that help them achieve success at school and in life.

It is easy to understand the first strand, that behaviour cannot be separated from the context where it occurs, by applying the principle to your own life.

Think about how you behave in your work situation.

What is your public demeanour? How do you dress and conduct yourself?

Now imagine yourself in a typical leisure situation: having a meal with friends, relaxing at home or playing tennis.

In what ways does the situation shape how you feel and behave?

If you no longer live in your original family (i.e. with your mother, father or primary caregiver) think about what happens to you when you return to your family home.

Does your behaviour change?

How does it change? Why?

Many people say that the instant they step over the threshold of their original family home they transform back into the child or the rebellious teenager they thought they had left far behind! Thinking about how you feel and act when you go back to your family home can give a potent example of how context shapes our behaviour.

Elements that shape our behaviour include values and expectations of a society that dictate how we behave, so we behave one way at a football match and another way at a family wedding. However, in addition, relationships shape our interactions and responses to the situation. For example, a mother–daughter relationship that is based on criticism will shape the dynamic two-way flow that influences each person. I have talked about the importance of context in shaping behaviour and in the following section I outline some contextual factors that influence classroom behaviours.

Children in context

Studies have shown that most troublesome behaviour is annoying rather than profoundly disturbing, but there is some evidence to suggest that teachers have to deal with more behaviour that shocks them. For example, one study (Hayden, 1997) found that teachers commented on the intensity and frequency of some behaviour that are emerging in classrooms.

Teachers say that they deal with more disturbed children than before, which reflects research that has identified increasing numbers of children at high-risk of educational and social failure. However, labelling children as high-risk can be a threat to healthy development in itself because it may increase teachers' potential to treat particular children differently or expect less from them.

Long-term studies show that often high-risk children grow into adults who experience many social, health and financial problems. Providing for the long-term needs of high-risk children causes a considerable burden to communities. Many high-risk children come from families experiencing life hazards including poverty, unemployment, poor housing, crowded living conditions, substance abuse and single parent households. These are all related to both child abuse and neglect, and juvenile crime (National Crime Prevention, 1999). Factors that contribute to children's high risk status include child maltreatment, divorce or marital strife, little support from extended families, social isolation and lack of high-quality extra-familial care (Pianta, 1999).

Experiencing life hazards, such as poverty, does not put children at high-risk automatically. There are many documented cases of children growing up in hazardous situations who achieve well. Researchers now think that educational and social achievement reflects warm, nurturing relationships with a caregiver, usually the mother.

Take some time now to reflect on your own childhood and the elements of the context that shaped your life. You may want to think about your family structure and the relatives who were important in your life:

- where you lived;
- the moves your family made;
- the occupation of the main breadwinner(s);
- family values and expectations;
- spiritual beliefs;
- the health and well-being of family members;
- the types of relationships between your parents, and your parents and yourself;
- your school experiences;
- your best friends;
- your best teacher;
- leisure activities of family members;
- external influences: political;
- community influences.

How did these elements contribute to the type of person you are today?

Thinking about the context in which you grew up can help you understand the factors that influenced who you are today: your hopes, dreams and aspirations for career, family, personal relationships, leisure, travel, home and finances. The type of people we are and the lives we lead is not just the luck of the gene pool, but shaped by our relationships with significant others.

Nurturing relationships protect children from harm and sustain them through challenging situations. However, children who grow up in hazardous contexts are more likely to experience unpredictable and unsafe home environments that provide few supportive relationships. At school, high-risk children have poor self-concepts and low social competence. They don't like themselves much and find it hard to get along with others, and they either attract a great deal of attention to themselves or become passive and withdrawn. Previously it was thought that children grow out of their problems but research has shown that the effects of insecure relationships are long lasting and pervasive (Pianta, 1999).

In sharp contrast to the children living in hazardous situations, many children experience safe, warm and nurturing relationships with their parents. Life has a consistent pattern for these children and the adults are dependable, firm and clear. There are sufficient resources for the family: money, food, clothing, housing and parents' time and attention.

The adults in these families tend to tell their children how they are expected to behave, and the adults' expectations are reasonable in terms of the child's developing competencies. Children may test out their parents and push against the boundaries that are set but they find that their parents' responses to their misdemeanours are predictable and reasonable. Above all, these children know that their parents will protect them from danger and threats to their well-being. These children know they are important in their parents' lives, and that their parents will always be there for them. The following section relates these ideas more closely to children's troublesome behaviours and provides a theoretical framework to guide thinking further.

The contextual systems model

Earlier I said that I would talk about some different ways of understanding children's behaviour. Teachers have every right to approach new ideas with suspicion because education has a long history of passing fads. Changes to conventional ways of thinking must be based on sound theory, and innovations that are plucked out of thin air should not convince professionals that the approach is valid and worth considering.

New approaches that are theoretically sound can help teachers make appropriate changes to their management of children's behaviour. Teachers who understand the theoretical basis of an approach can use it as part of their accountability practices when talking about their management strategies to their principal or the children's parents.

The following section gives an overview of Pianta and Walsh's (1996, pp. 62–72) contextual systems model (CSM) (which I will refer to as the 'systems model') which is the theoretical basis of this book. Readers seeking a detailed explanation of the model should consult Pianta and Walsh (1996), where the authors explain that the CSM is drawn from developmental systems theory based on Ford and Lerner's (1992) work, and Sameroff (1983; 1989). The systems model helps us to map the relationship between child, family and school that creates contexts for children's behaviour, and it helps to clarify the systems of relations and their subordinate systems. Figure 1.1 is a simple diagram that shows some of the systems that can influence children's classroom behaviour (Pianta and Walsh, 1996).

The systems shown in Figure 1.1 have many interrelated components that may influence children's behaviour, and they include:

- the government policies that mandate education funding;
- the bureaucracy that direct funding to schools;
- system-wide policies governing curriculum and assessment;
- system-wide support personnel;
- management who implement policies;
- personnel who provide a range of services to the school, including school health nurse, receptionist, canteen manager, librarian, specialist, school psychologist, cleaners, gardener;
- the teaching staff;
- the buildings, space, playground, furniture, fittings, resources and supplies;
- the maintenance system to clean and take care of the school;
- the parents and families;
- the curriculum;
- the timetable;
- school rules and policies to maintain them;
- the children.

Each element of the system facilitates the efficient functioning of the school. Schools operate effectively with appropriate buildings, resources or equipment. They operate well with good support staff who provide valuable services and they would not operate without children. However, each component of the system is a system itself. The child is a system and families are a system. You, the teacher, are a system made up from your personality, experience, education, expectations and values. How can systems theory help a teacher who wants to help children achieve their potentials? Having a system view can help you identify the factors that you can control and change, which can lead to identifying effective ways to change.

Systems and education

The school is a unit with considerable power to regulate the behaviour of the teachers and children. However, that is not the end of the story. As Figure 1.1 shows, many schools are managed by a bureaucracy, which receives its directives from the government.

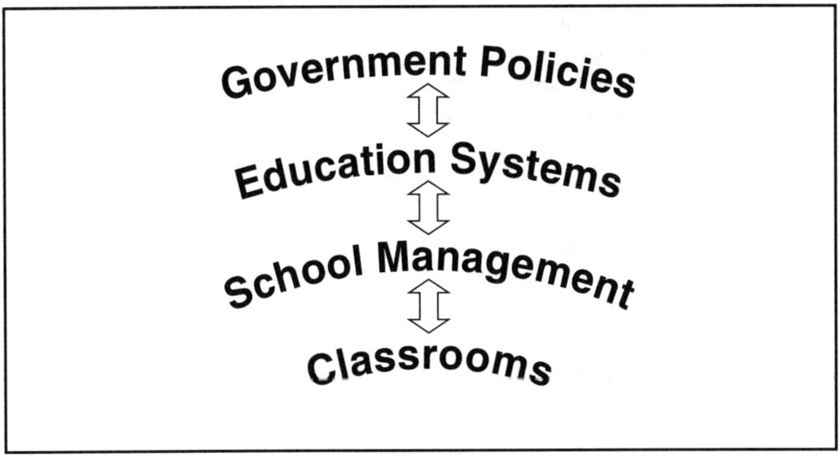

Figure 1.1 Systems that influence children's behaviours.

Think about the governance of the schools you work in and identify some specific examples that show the links between government policies, the education bureaucracy, school system and children's behaviour.

Government policy controls finance to schools, which has a direct impact on schools' decisions. Economic decisions dictate the materials, equipment and personnel in schools, which can have a major impact on the practices in the school. Dedicated and effective teachers enable educational reform to be implemented and foster high standards in education.

A systems view of education can help teachers to advocate for better policies and more public awareness of the complexity of teaching. A systems view could help teachers identify the support they need from bureaucracies and pinpoint more quickly the causes of increases in problematic behaviours.

Systems and communities

Systems are embedded within various cultural and sub-cultural contexts that influence the child and family. Each element creates a context for children's social and education progress through interaction with the child–family relationships. The contexts that provide opportunities to children and encourage school success include:

- government support agencies;
- home–school liaison and support services;

- child care and after-school care services;
- employment opportunities;
- neighbourhood and community resources;
- extended family and support networks;
- medical services;
- spiritual and charitable organisations;

Each one of these systems provides threats and opportunities for children's growth and well being. For example, high-quality childcare provides opportunities for children's physical, social, emotional and intellectual development. Employment that offers the primary breadwinner in the family a good wage and fulfilling work provides an opportunity for increases to the family's sense of wellness.

Systems and schools

Applying the system's model to schools means seeing each classroom as a system, as well as every child and teacher. At the same time the management structure is a system, as are the support services. The qualifications, experiences, skills, talents and motivations of the staff are an important element of the school system, and the qualities of leadership are pivotal in the system.

In this book, no attempt is made to say, 'This is *the* way, the one and only way' to help children achieve their potentials because the context of each school is different. There are obvious differences in:

- school staff – levels of experience, education, personalities, skills, talents, interests, and family situations;
- school buildings – and access to space, materials, equipment, specialist services, rooms and sporting facilities;
- school populations – children, families, changes and stability within families, extended families, ethnicity and culture, racial origins; socio-economic level, employment, health, leisure and sporting interests – hobbies and relaxation.

Investigating children's troublesome behaviour may begin at the classroom level but often has to extend to the school level, as children's relationships in the playground, canteen, library, music and art rooms are important influences in their behaviour.

The classroom system and troublesome behaviour

Teachers' difficulties with classroom behaviours are influenced by educational reform, how the school tackles inappropriate behaviour, and how the teacher thinks about it and responds to it. Once the teacher is behind closed classroom doors then meanings about behaviour are constructed and negotiated between the teacher and children in an ongoing process. A classroom is a system, as is the child and the teacher. Applying the systems model to classrooms can help teachers to understand that troublesome behaviours:

- result from many factors that interact over time;
- develop from repeated interactions and relationships between factors;
- can be interpreted in many ways depending on different perspectives.

In classrooms, children have relationships with space, materials, equipment, peers, teachers and support staff. Children's home experiences lead them to expect certain things from their relationships with adults and they will behave in ways that fit their expectations.

Contexts support relationships as they:

- shape and are shaped by individuals, tools, resources, intentions and ideas;
- are fluid and dynamic, and constantly in the process of change;
- are social because they reflect and frame interactions.

The underlying issues will be explored in the following chapter in order to foster evidence-based practices that can change difficult situations.

Summary

This chapter has presented the theoretical framework that underpins the book. I have suggested that systems theory provides an appropriate framework to consider children's troublesome behaviour. Systems theory can help teachers develop different understandings that will help them create schools where children and teachers enjoy learning together. The following chapters apply the systems framework to explore troublesome behaviour from the perspectives of teachers, children and schools.

Chapter 2

Focus on learning relationships

This chapter explores the idea that developing good learning relationships in the classroom is one of the most critical aspects of teaching (Evans, 1996). A focus of this chapter concerns how children's behaviours reflect relationships with their teacher, peers and context. The chapter asks you to reflect on troublesome behaviour by thinking about learning and behaving as integrated components of the classroom rather than fragmented attributes of the child.

This chapter discusses the dilemmas faced by some children in classrooms that incorporate active learning strategies. As you read the chapter I would like you to consider how relationships make a difference in your classroom and what you can do to foster learning relationships.

Appropriate classroom behaviours

Teachers have clear ideas about their ideal student, and the behaviours they like to see in classrooms. Well-adjusted children who get along well with others seem to manage life in classrooms with ease. Many teachers say that children behave well when they follow the teacher's instructions quickly and smoothly, keep to the routines and look after their possessions. Complying with the classroom rules, being in the right place at the right time and getting on with work by themselves, will see most children through the school day without trouble.

The children who are judged to behave well seem to understand how the classroom works, appear content to go with the flow, and keep themselves on track with some recognition for their efforts from time to time. By contrast, children get into trouble when they:

- are slow to follow the teacher's instructions, appear to forget instructions, or refuse to follow instructions;
- talk out of turn – interrupt the teacher/peers, call out, talk to others at the wrong time;
- move around the room inappropriately;

- lose/forget/damage their pencils, books, clothing, equipment, which means they can't get on with their learning tasks;
- do not settle to work or complete learning tasks;
- prevent others from learning by talking to them, touching them, or interfering with their books, materials, and equipment.

As the list shows, children get into trouble when they disrupt the flow of teaching and learning in ways that demand teacher attention.

Scan the list of inappropriate behaviours.

Do you agree that they are common causes of concern in classrooms? Do you want to add or delete any from the list?

If you do, try to specify your reason.

What behaviours cause you concern in the classroom?

Making your own list would help you to make your expectations explicit and help you to work out what behaviour you value and reinforce.

Talking over the list with colleagues would be helpful. Listening to other people's views will help you understand how ideas about children's behaviour vary, and how they influence classroom practice.

There is little doubt that the teacher can monitor behaviour closely and impose greater control on the group when children are seated in rows and engaged in whole-class activities. It is much easier to pick out the one or two children who have not followed an instruction in traditional primary school classrooms. Locating noise, scanning the class, and monitoring progress is easier when all children are engaged in the same piece of work at the same time. Changes in education however, mean that teachers are no longer encouraged to manage their classes in the traditional way. Many education systems expect teachers to use active learning strategies for at least some part of the day.

Changes to teaching and learning

In the past, a great deal of teaching was based on the belief that children learnt when teachers transmitted knowledge effectively and allowed children to practice and refine their knowledge or skill. Transmission-based teaching fits behavioural models of learning but not active learning. Behavioural models emphasise that teachers define knowledge that children learn, which can be measured as a commodity or product.

Newer research shows that children learn when they have opportunities to make sense of new information by engaging actively with it and often this means through first-hand experience and social interaction (Gauvain, 1998). Learning occurs most powerfully when learners take in and use information to build on and extend their understandings about their world. Valuable learning experiences allow children to integrate new experiences with familiar ones by constructing and refining knowledge schemes in an ongoing process (Marlowe and Page, 1998, p. 10).

Children learn by interacting with peers and adults, as well as materials, equipment, tools and events. Children construct meaning through the process of explaining their ideas, debating issues and negotiating understandings. Interacting with others gives children opportunities to make sense of the world and store meanings in their long-term memories. These meanings can be retrieved later and then generalised and applied to novel materials and situations. Often, this model of how children learn is referred to as 'active learning'.

Implementing active learning strategies means that classrooms are dynamic places where learners move, talk, investigate their ideas, negotiate and problem solve, which means that the teacher has far less control of the children as a class group. The new understandings of ways in which children learn mean that ideas about teaching have had to change.

Teaching for active learning

Teachers who adopt active learning approaches provide experiences that look very different from traditional tasks. The emphasis on 'sitting and listening' is balanced with opportunities to build schemes of knowledge in an active and interactive process of discovering answers, solutions, concepts and links between knowledge schemes. Teaching in these active learning situations has been described as 'assisted performance' (Tharp and Gallimore, 1998).

Interest in teaching for active learning has grown with the emergence of outcomes-based education in many contexts. Teachers may have less control over the learning outcomes that students achieve because they use their thinking processes to develop, build and alter meanings and understandings that they integrate with experiences and existing knowledge (Marlowe and Page, 1998). Teaching for active learning means that many ideas about effective teaching have had to change, and some of these changes are summarised in Figure 2.1.

Many teachers have responded enthusiastically to the principles of active learning and adapted their teaching strategies to take account of new ideas about how children learn curriculum content. Teachers have endeavoured to teach in ways that help children explore and act on materials, equipment, tools and new situations, create, try out innovations and solve problems collaboratively. But schools have found that unexpected difficulties create roadblocks to active learning practices (Horsch, Chen and Nelson, 1999).

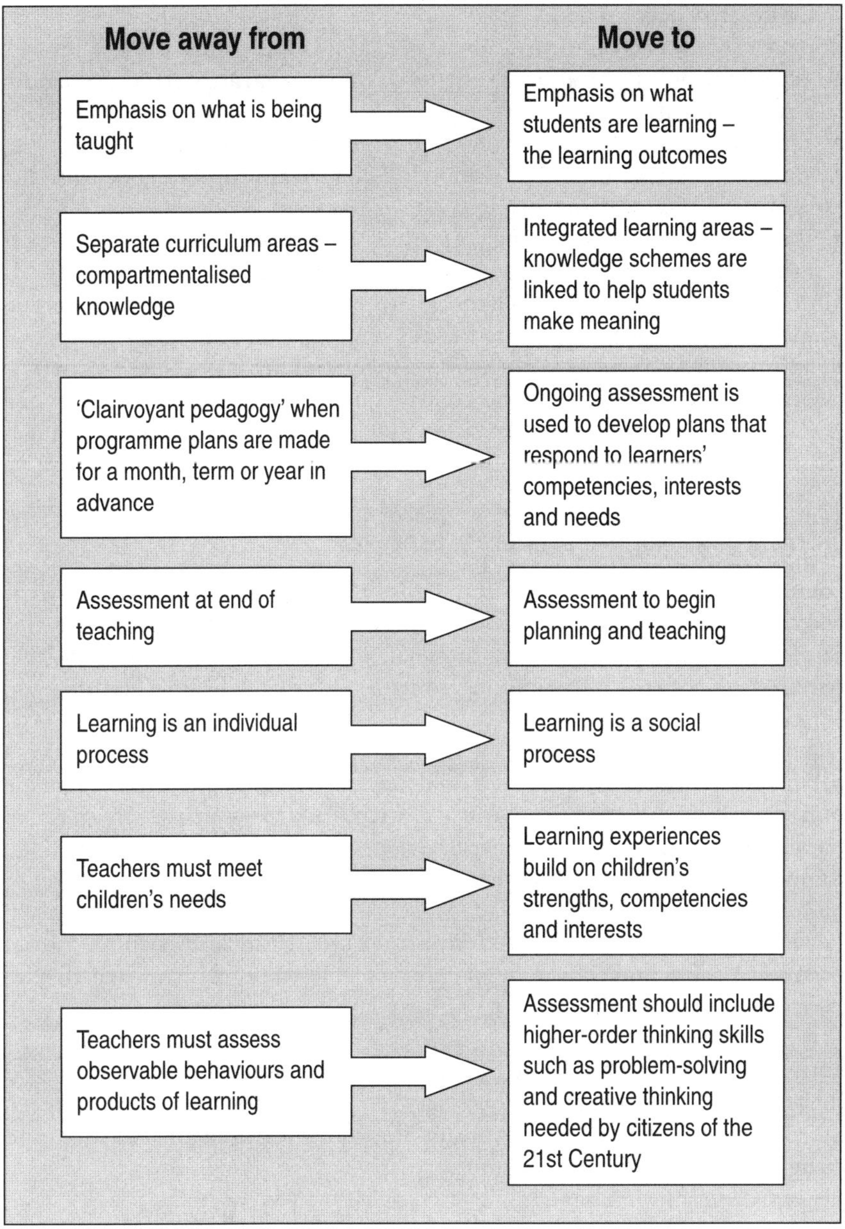

Figure 2.1 Changes to teaching and learning.

Difficulties occur when:

- curriculum is thought about as if it is separate from classroom management;
- teachers don't identify the new behaviours that active learning requires;
- teachers assume that all children will behave appropriately because the learning tasks are interesting;
- teachers don't envisage that they need to facilitate the new behaviours that children need in active learning situations;
- there are clashes in values between ideas about empowering children to learn and expecting them to behave in compliant and passive ways;
- education systems have particular expectations that pressure teachers to make decisions against their better judgements, for example, when children have to achieve specified outcomes at particular ages or stages of education.

Learning outcomes and individuals' behaviour

Some teachers work in education systems that direct their practice in specific ways and they may have little room to move within the system's requirements. These teachers may think that they can only cope with the system-level required outcomes by maintaining control over the children's learning and behaviour.

Learning tasks mandated by the education systems may promote a behavioural approach because children needed to acquire prescribed learning outcomes and predetermined ends. Difficulties arise when teachers try to implement active learning *and* meet the demands of the mandated curriculum, for example one teacher said that:

> It's like fitting square pegs into round holes. Pressure is coming from above the school. Now pupils are not able to do things when they're ready but when they need to be tested ...

Trying to get children ready to perform well on assessment tasks increased the teachers' stress levels. Teachers may feel they had to help children reach the required standard, which meant imposing learning on children and clamping down on their behaviour.

Teaching children as individuals

Part of teachers' difficulties comes from the belief that they should teach children as individuals. This is embedded deeply as a philosophical ideal that does not fit well with newer conceptions of learning. Teachers think they should be able to treat a class of thirty children as individuals, and many of them feel guilty when they find it is an impossible task. One teacher said she felt inadequate because she believed good teachers:

> ... are aware of each pupil and their individual stage of development
> ... and they have individual plans for them

Both experienced and newly qualified teachers accept the doctrine of individualism without question, and one teacher said that if only they could do it better they would achieve the ideal. One young teacher talked about wanting to teach children as individuals and made the poignant comment that she didn't manage it very well and said, '*I just feel like I'm failing*'.

Teachers rarely question the practical reality of planning for and teaching thirty individuals. For example, they may struggle to find the balance between treating children as individuals, fostering small group work and maintaining a consistent set of rules and routines that experts in classroom management say are essential.

The goal of teaching thirty children as individuals is an unworkable ideal that:

- perpetuates criticisms of teachers;
- fosters teachers' doubts about their efficacy and professionalism;
- does not match the principles of small group learning/collaborative learning in today's classrooms.

Teachers need to develop supportive relationships with individual children but it is more helpful to see behaviour as belonging to the learning context rather than the individual.

Competing demands: learning and behaving

When teachers try to implement active learning strategies without thinking through issues for children's behaviour, then there may be increases in troublesome behaviour. One problem is that children may experience two competing sets of demands for learning and behaving. Encouraging children to be active learners may not fit well with requiring children to be compliant students.

Some teachers found that children responded to the new ways of learning with increased troublesome behaviour, which was associated with large class sizes and children who were multi-lingual with a range of social, emotional and academic problems (Horsch, Chen and Nelson, 1999). Often active learning seeks to engage children in collaborative problem-solving tasks that requires them to give instructions to their peers, reflect on the group process, respond to peer questions and challenges, and pose questions and challenges to others (Forman and Cazden, 1988). Some children have difficulties with these learning processes and may cover up their confusions with increased episodes of troublesome behaviour.

Teachers may be at a loss to know how to respond to behaviour problems, and their difficulties increase when they feel unsupported in their school context. School leaders may say they support active learning but expect teachers to ensure that children behave in quiet and passive ways. How might the difference between teaching for active learning and managing behaviour be talked about in schools? One principal talked about her support for active learning but expressed different ideas about children's behaviour. The principal emphasised that an active learning approach was school policy that teachers could not change:

> Children ought to be active learners who construct their knowledge from first-hand experiences, which describes the way that this school is run – it's implicit. Teachers are not free to teach in a style of teaching that doesn't involve children as active learners.

However, later when talking about children's troublesome classroom behaviour the principal explained:

> The issue is force of personality of the teacher, and whether the teacher is established with the group, and whether teachers can impose themselves on the pupils enough to keep control of the situation ... teachers must keep one step ahead and control the situation.

The principal had a firm commitment to the active learning approach to academic content with its implication of the teacher as a partner in children's learning, but insisted that the teacher should maintain power to control children's behaviour. She did not indicate that there was a problem between these two sets of knowledge. Look again at the principal's comments and you will see that she described teachers' behaviour in terms of power, saying teachers must:

- ... impose themselves on the pupils ...
- ... (have) force of personality...
- ... keep one step ahead (of the children)
- ... control the situation.

This language reveals the image of top-down power being imposed on the children by keeping *one step ahead* that is at odds with the idea of the teacher working side-by-side with empowered children. A teacher who has to impose the *force of personality* on children is unlikely to value children's ideas and respond to them.

You might be surprised that the principal could hold two different and competing sets of knowledge without realising that they were incompatible.

This situation occurs when staff do not collaborate to clarify their meanings or talk through their understandings, so that contradictions are not made explicit.

Teachers may be trying to achieve the impossible by expecting children to be active learners, but behave according to traditional ways. The clash between empowering children as learners and maintaining control over their behaviour will result in unnecessary stress. Keeping the principal happy by having the classroom look normal in traditional terms, at the same time as implementing active learning strategies is likely to be too demanding for teachers and children.

Active learning asks children to be self-motivated and collaborate with others to construct their knowledge. Children use adults and peers as resources to scaffold their understanding by asking questions and seeking alternative answers. Teachers using active learning strategies implement Vygotsky's notions of working within the children's zones of proximal development (zoped) (Addison Stone, 1998). In order to work within a child's zoped, the teacher identifies the learning that children can achieve alone and the learning they can achieve working with a more knowledgeable other; either a peer or adult (Addison Stone, 1998). The distance (or zone) between the two points represents the zone of proximal development.

Teachers might be keen to adopt new approaches to teaching that maximise children's opportunities to learn through interacting with their peers. These teachers' classrooms are full of the movement, talk and activity associated with collaborative approaches to learning. The teacher adopts different roles during active learning experiences, which are described by Moll and Whitmore (1998) as:

1 guide and supporter – the teacher helps the children to focus their questions and ideas and supports them into activities that will lead to academic success;
2 active participant in learning – the teacher does not know the answers before posing questions but investigates the answers with the children;
3 evaluator– the teacher assesses and evaluates children's growth and learning as individuals and as a group;
4 facilitator – the teacher plans the classroom context to promote learning, language and literacy.

You will see from the list that the teaching roles require different sets of skills and knowledge that teachers try out as they implement the new learning tasks. However, the new tasks require different skills and knowledge from children as well, and the list above does not include teacher as *mediator* of disputes or *coach* of new behaviours, which may be essential to successful active learning tasks (Baker-Sennett, Matusov and Rogoff, 1998).

Teachers may realise that troublesome behaviours increase partly because not all children are self-motivated learners who can work collaboratively.

Teachers may respond by increasing their control over children's behaviours while attempting to encourage active learning. Some teachers become concerned about the increased levels of noise, chatter and activity, which do not fit well with their images of a well-run classroom. Some teachers worry about what their teaching colleagues think of them, or that the principal will think they lack control of the class.

One difficulty with teaching for active learning is that the strategies don't align with techniques to manage behaviour that worked quite well when children sat at desks in rows, doing the same work at the same time. Many teachers were trained to manage their classrooms according to the behavioural model:

> Gold stars, smarties in the jar, and praise, praise, praise.

Teachers experience difficulties when they try to build a collaborative community of learners at the same time as applying management techniques that emphasise competition and compliance.

Many teachers need help to think through the issues of classroom management that the new ways of teaching and learning provoke. The move away from transmission-based teaching to constructivist teaching means that classrooms will look, sound and feel different from traditional classrooms. Some differences between the active learning model and the behavioural model are seen in Figure 2.2, which compares the attributes of active learners with the attributes of children who behave well.

As you see in Figure 2.2, the good learners list means that children *collaborate* with peers and adults to construct knowledge and understandings, while the good behaviour list requires children to *cooperate* with the teacher. The two sets of behaviours may result in incongruent messages being received by vulnerable children who struggle to decode them. It has been said that teaching for understanding at the same time as managing for compliance will not work (McCaslin and Good, 1998).

Do you agree that 'active learning' may result in expecting two competing sets of behaviours in classrooms?

What behaviours are rewarded in schools in your context?

Try and give some specific examples of teaching strategies for academic learning and some strategies for guiding children's behaviour in order to decide how well they match.

Some children may find that the two sets of behaviours present increasing levels of uncertainty that are too difficult for them to manage. There is little doubt that active learning approaches create many opportunities for children

Collaborative Learning	*Cooperative Behaviour*
• Interact with peers/adults to construct knowledge, often in small groups;	• Complete the teacher's set tasks by working independently;
• Interact with others by posing questions, negotiating meanings, problem solving, constructing creative solutions;	• Speak when the teacher gives permission; • Answer questions posed by the teacher;
• Act on materials and equipment with others in creative ways;	• Follow teacher's instructions quickly and quietly;
• Are risk-takers, who pursue their interests, and build on their strengths and competencies with others.	• Keep the rules and routines of the classroom.

Figure 2.2 Collaborative learners and cooperative behaviours.

to behave in ways that disrupt the flow of teaching and learning. Some children find it difficult to read and interpret the cues intended to help them engage in the learning tasks (Green and Weade, 1985). These children may respond by making unreasonable demands on the teacher's time; being scatty and disorganised; being slow to start and finish tasks; being irritable and on the brink of blowing a short fuse. Some children may find the freedom to exercise choice, make decisions and follow their interests very challenging, particularly if they have experienced several years in a traditional teacher-directed classroom.

Some children find it difficult to self-regulate their learning, motivation and behaviour and may not feel comfortable in learner-oriented classrooms (McCaslin and Good, 1998). It is unfortunate that behaviour difficulties are likely to emerge at the same time as the teacher is learning new skills of teaching for active learning. It is not hard to imagine that teachers may feel overwhelmed by the extra demands that additional troublesome behaviours make on them. They may try to ignore inappropriate behaviours but may find that children escalate the behaviours apparently to provoke a response.

Teachers may respond to children's increased troublesome behaviours by giving up the innovative ways of teaching and learning and go back to greater teacher control and direction. Teachers may decide that the newer active learning approaches are not practical and go for safer but less satisfying options that include individual seatwork and greater control. Another response is to change teaching methods, but continue to try to manage the classroom for control, narrow obedience and compliance (McCaslin and Good, 1992). A third option is for the teacher to work in the child's zone of proximal development (zoped) to scaffold the behaviours needed by active learners, and this approach is the focus of the following section. Active learning requires teachers to use advanced management approaches that involve different kinds of teacher control, aimed at promoting trust relationships that are embedded in the learning community (McCaslin and Good, 1998).

Scaffolding behaviours for active learners

Teachers have welcomed active learning in the classroom, but they understand that they need to learn some different ways of interacting with children. These teachers are eager to expand their teaching repertoires to help children develop the emotional and social skills they need to be effective learners in today's classrooms. Applying the active learning perspective helps teachers to understand how the social context influences children's thoughts and actions (Bloom, Permutter and Burrell, 1999). The constructivist perspective encourages teachers to create a sense of community that embraces all children, and supports them to develop the skills of conflict resolution and self-regulation needed to function effectively.

Importantly, teachers recognise that the types of relationships that develop in traditional classrooms are different from the relationships in active learning classrooms. Developing trust relationships with students is the essence of success, as satisfying social interactions help to promote children's feelings of self-worth and self-efficacy (Bloom, Permutter and Burrell, 1999). A key point is that relationships are a 'zone of proximal development' (Vygotsky, 1934/1986) for children's behaviour, which offers opportunities and constraints for growth.

Active learning requires children to use a set of relationship skills that include:

- listening to others;
- responding to others' ideas;
- initiating ideas;
- negotiating with others;
- problem-solving;
- working together in fair and equitable ways.

Kohn (1991 p. 51) describes carefully structured collaborative learning as 'essentially humanising experiences', that help children to consider others and encourages trust, sensitivity, and open communication. Many children watch these relationship skills being modelled by their parents and they experience them first-hand in their families and in their classrooms. However, some children have few opportunities to develop these skills because they experience difficult family relationships.

Some children know that the only way you get what you want is to be bigger, louder and more threatening than others. These children have had little experience in negotiating or problem-solving and their skills may not develop quickly. Many children will not develop these skills by osmosis, for example, just by being in a particular context and being exposed to them.

Vulnerable children may get lost in active learning situations. Trying to engage in small group collaboration without the necessary set of skills would be akin to negotiating a foreign city without a road map. How do children learn to work together, compromise or problem-solve with their peers if they have had little practice in these skills? These children may respond with behaviours that disrupt teaching and learning.

Teachers may assume that children will acquire certain skills by observing the role model of their peers. Some children might learn the skills in this way, but others will not. If children cannot learn the necessary skills by observing others, then it is likely that they will cover up their difficulties and distract the teacher by behaving inappropriately. These children need direct intervention to help them acquire collaborative learning skills to be successful active learners.

Difficulties might be experienced by children entering preschool or primary school and being faced with a range of social demands that are new to them. These children may begin to display uncompliant behaviour in their efforts to solve social problems and avoid learning tasks that they don't understand (Van Acker and Talbott, 1999). Teachers who do not help children learn appropriate behaviours may find that there is an increase in refusal to comply with teacher directives, increased aggressive behaviour and increases in peer rejection (Van Acker and Talbott, 1999).

One problem is that teachers have been taught to identify children's zones of proximal development (zoped) in the *cognitive* domain but not in the *psychosocial* domain (Pianta, 1999). The psychosocial domain includes:

- knowing how to behave in different situations and with different groups of people;
- being able to delay gratification, compromise at times, be cooperative for the sake of the group, and help to ensure the classroom runs smoothly;
- making and keeping friends;
- getting help when you need it;
- having a positive self-concept;
- having a realistic view of one's competencies.

Teachers who work in children's psychosocial domain ask, 'What can she do now? What does she need to learn to do next? How can I help her learn this new skill?' Teachers have the option to work in children's zones of proximal development in the psychosocial domain in order to help children develop the skills central to the learning tasks.

Stimulation and appropriate curriculum is necessary for children struggling with classroom behaviour, particularly for those who have had a poor start to school learning. Learning problems quickly lead some children to mask their difficulties with difficult behaviour. These children lose motivation, refuse to complete set tasks and may use aggressive behaviour to avoid the tasks they find hard (Van Acker and Talbott, 1999).

Teachers can take steps to overcome some of the barriers to active learning when they use instructional strategies that foster both academic and social learning goals by coaching of prosocial behaviour within academic content (Van Acker and Talbott, 1999). For example, a physical education session designed to teach ball-handling skills can be structured to facilitate turn taking, working in a small group and being collaborative. Teachers who recognise that these skills are important can take steps to reinforce them, coach them, scaffold them and celebrate with children when they use them.

Child–child relationships

Studies have found links between peer relationships and children's classroom behaviour (Howes and Hamilton, 1992). Teachers cannot afford to ignore the social relationships in the classroom, as there is nothing neat about relationships which tend to be unpredictable and changeable. One important principle is that relationships always exist between units in the system even when it appears that there is none. For example, a child may never be observed to interact with his peers, but this does not mean that relationships do not exist between them, or that relationships are not influencing the child's behaviour.

Spend some time thinking about the following example to get an idea of how working in a child's zoped might work out in practice. Try to work through the steps listed below. Ask yourself:

- What can the child do by himself?
- What can he do with the teacher's support?
- What is he likely to be able to learn next?

The teacher may identify that a child can work collaboratively with a more knowledgeable partner but not in a small group. Having attended to any contextual factors that might be contributing to Carlo's difficulties (such as the provision of equipment, space and time), the teacher would:

The teacher was pleased to see Carlo working well on the science experiment with his partner, as this situation had created difficulties in the past. She could see them talking to one another, sharing equipment and discussing solutions to the problem. She decided to allow two other children to join the table, as there was plenty of room. But a few minutes later there were some angry voices and pushing and shoving from that end of the room. It seemed that Carlo had lost his patience with the newcomers and attempted to reclaim the equipment by grabbing it off them.

1 What had gone wrong?
2 What situation did Carlo manage?
3 What situation did he find difficult?

4 What other information does the teacher need? For example, did Carlo's partner and the two newcomers do anything to provoke or respond negatively to Carlo?
5 What did the context do to provoke or respond to Carlo? For example, was there enough space, equipment and time for collaborative activities?
6 Identify Carlo's zone of proximal development (zoped).
7 How could the teacher use the zoped to scaffold important skills?
8 What steps do you recommend his teacher to take?

- *move* the child to partner work, making sure that the peer is able to model appropriate behaviour;
- *support* the child and be on hand to model, coach and teach skills, such as turn-taking, listening, and respecting others' views;
- *reinforce* the skills when Carlo exhibits them;
- *gradually lessen* the support as Carlo internalises the skills and increase the group size to three and then four;
- *participate* in the group intermittently until teacher support is no longer required and the child is functioning well.

It is suggested that this scaffolding technique could be used to support a range of skills needed when children engage in constructivist learning experiences. It is just as important to spend time helping the child in the zone of proximal development for classroom behaviours as it is for cognitive development.

Identifying children's zoped and scaffolding certain behaviour will:

- help each child learn the skills needed for success, thus meeting social justice issues;
- ensure that the teacher begins with the child's competencies and builds on them;
- free up the teacher's time and energy;
- foster more positive classroom relationships and a positive learning environment.

Teachers get a different perspective of behaviour when they see that teaching and learning cannot be separated from children's relationships with their peers and teacher. Each child adapts to the opportunities provided by the context that stimulate the child's development further (Pianta and Walsh, 1996). Children interact with the context and adapt to the context through their relationships, and these ideas are discussed in the following section.

Teacher–child relationships

Teachers might ask how understanding the systems model will help them in the classroom when faced with an uncompliant child who has experienced life hazards. Understanding systems is likely to alter the cognitions that teachers develop about children who exhibit troublesome behaviours and they will be alert to idea that they need to investigate aspects of the context that might not be supporting the child's development.

Teacher–child relationships influence children's developing skills in peer relations, social skills and self-regulation, and help to reduce levels of risk for some children (Pianta, 1999). Relationships with children enrich teachers' lives, but they bring responsibilities. Teachers need to ensure that children are protected from psychological and physical harm, and they have to nurture children's rights to learn and develop. These responsibilities mean that teachers must deal with troublesome behaviours and help vulnerable children learn life skills that will enable them to be competent members of society.

It would be a mistake to think that relationships develop in an orderly fashion, or that one interaction leads to a particular consequence. For example, it may be incorrect to claim that a teacher's harshness to a child on a particular day made the child behave in an anti-social way. The child's behaviour is more likely to result from a complex set of interactions over time between child and teacher which lead both parties to expect and predict certain things. Pianta and Walsh (1996) explain that histories provide us with fast-forward and feedback loops:

> Fast-forward – '*I just know that this kid will kick up a stink*'
> Feedback – '*... because the last time this happened with this type of child ...*'

Time is an important element in the systems model, which highlights the developmental aspect of behaviour. Time or history affects the child's behaviour, which means that teachers may not be able to explain a child's troublesome behaviours by using only current knowledge of the child. Observations of a child in a classroom cannot take into account the interactions between systems over time that provided the context for the child's development. Similarly, observing a child in classroom does not give information about a child's experiences in the playground or the football field that may have an effect on behaviour in class.

Research shows that some children who exhibit troublesome classroom behaviour have experienced social relationships that hamper their capacity to experience school success. A great deal of research has established links between social factors and achievement at school, for example, relationships between children and adults influence:

- early school achievements (Pianta, 1997);
- peer relations (Howes, Hamilton, and Matheson, 1994);
- school competencies such as attention, motivation, problem solving and self-esteem (Birch and Ladd, 1997).

The following case describes relationship dynamics that could lead to negative long-term effects for one child. As you read the case, try to relate to a child that you have taught. What would you do to help this child?

> Errol's teacher identified him as a 'loner' who participated rarely in small-group learning experiences with his peers. The teacher found Errol to be very quiet and said that he did not have the social skills of the other children in his class. Observations in the classroom supported the teacher's observations, as Errol seemed to avoid contact with other children, and apparently preferred to work alone.
>
> However observations over three weeks in the playground provided some important additional information indicating Errol was a rejected child rather than an isolate. Observations showed that Errol's approaches tended to be rebuffed by other children, and that children sought him out to reject him. A typical example was observed when Errol was playing outside with Jesse. Errol grabbed Jesse's arm and swung him to the ground. Jesse appeared to be upset and walked away. Errol watched him go, and then went to sit inside a cement tunnel by himself. Another child, Nicholas, went into the tunnel, put his thumbs in his ears and wriggled his fingers in a teasing fashion at Errol, who watched him and did not respond. Then Nicholas spat on the ground next to Errol and walked away. Errol walked to the veranda and sat at the table that had play dough on it. He manipulated the dough alone, until the teacher called for all the children to go inside (Corrie and Leitao, 1999).

Later conversations with the teacher showed that she did not know about the playground dynamics that were influencing Errol's behaviour in the classroom. The teacher was dismayed by the other children's treatment of Errol, and asked how she could help him develop the skills he needed to deal with such situations. Notice that the teacher assumed that:

- Errol lacked skills;
- these skills could be taught.

The fact that Errol had seldom been seen to interact positively with others might mislead the teacher to think that he lacked social skills. However, the teacher needs to consider if the classroom and playground were providing opportunities for Errol to exhibit particular skills.

When considering the steps to take to change the negative relationship that had developed between Errol and his peers, the teacher needed to understand the effects of time and history on the relationships. The teacher may want to think about the ways in which Errol's social skills could not be separated from the context in which they occurred. The following questions could be used as a starting point, and some may stimulate information gathering to ensure that answers are evidence-based:

- Is rejection/inclusion part of the norms of the classroom context? Has the group rejected other children besides Errol? For example, children with poorly developed sports skills might be rejected in a class or school where sporting prowess brings high status and competition is fostered;
- What are Errol's interests and competencies? How can I ensure that he has an opportunity to maximise them? How can I use his interests and competencies to help him develop positive relationships with his peers?
- How do I feel and behave towards Errol? Do I include him during whole group times? Do I invite him to participate in games or activities, for example, to pick a song or do the calendar? Do I give him recognition for his learning tasks? Do I support and encourage him?
- Am I as friendly and positive with him as with other children? Do I notice him when he arrives? Do I greet him and farewell him warmly or have I responded to his early coolness towards me by backing off?
- What's my relationship with Errol's family? Do I talk to his mother when she comes to collect him? How does Errol's mother respond to me? What do I know about his family and his early experiences?
- What dynamics in the playground might be contributing to the group's behaviour?
- What could be changed to facilitate healthier relationships? For example, is there enough equipment outside for children to share? Could equipment be place differently to facilitate sharing? Could I put out different equipment or provide other activities that provoke collaboration?
- Have I given children opportunities to talk about playground difficulties or friendship? Do children need more guidance about friendships – getting friends and keeping friends, joining the game, keeping the rules and leaving the game?

Teachers who seek objective information to the type of questions listed above are enacting roles as teacher-researchers. Seeking information about the system of relationships between the child and the context removes the focus away from the individual child and can lead to change.

Errol's teacher was right to be concerned about his situation in the group as research shows that the effects of children's relationships are long-lasting and influence children's social adjustment as adults (Asher and Coie, 1990). Social rejection by the peer group is a major stress that leads to loneliness and anger. Children who were rejected in kindergarten are much more likely to have conduct disorders three years later (Dodge, 1996).

What influences some children to develop easy and fulfilling peer relationships, while others do not? Some research suggests that children's later relationships are shaped by their early experiences that begin at birth (Howes, Hamilton and Matheson, 1994). The following section explores these ideas and draws on research to link children's early relationship experiences with those they develop in the classroom.

Parent–child relationships

It is necessary for survival that infants connect with a person who will comfort, nurture and protect them, and this person is usually the infant's mother or primary caregiver. For ease, in this discussion I refer to the primary caregiver as the mother, although many children form secure attachment relationships with a primary caregiver who is not their mother, and some primary caregivers are male. The relationship that develops between the child and mother is known as the 'attachment relationship' (see Ainsworth, Blehar, Waters and Wall, 1978; Crittenden, 1992).

If a mother does not respond to the infant's needs appropriately, then the infant will strive to arouse the mother's attachment behaviour. The infant will develop strategies to gain attention and care in either adaptive or maladaptive ways that respond to the mother's caring, rejecting or inconsistent behaviours (Cassidy, 1999).

Children's early experiences and their relationships with their primary caregiver reinforce aspects of their personality and for some children this is a nurturing experience filled with love. Other children may experience clashes between their disposition and their parents' personalities and it may lead to long-term difficulties if their parents cannot adapt. For example, when a 'lively wriggler' is born to parents who are placid types, the parents need to adapt their understandings of what is normal behaviour. If parents do not adapt to their active and enthusiastic child, they may begin to wonder 'What's wrong with this child?'

Children who experience appropriate love and nurture are likely to develop secure attachment relationships with their mothers. Children who receive inadequate or inconsistent love and nurture are likely to develop insecure attachment relationships (Crittenden, 1992). As a result of their early experiences with their mother, children develop internal representations or cognitions about relationships, which guide their expectations about their future relationships (Crittenden, 1992).

Securely attached infants grow into children who:

- have high feelings of self-worth;
- have a robust sense of self;
- are self-reliant;
- develop autonomy;
- have a good sense of their personal power;
- have a positive view of the world;

- are competent in their relationships with peers and adults; (Cassidy and Shaver, 1999; Fonagy *et al.*, 1997; Howes, Hamilton and Matheson, 1994).

By contrast, insecurely attached infants grow into children who doubt themselves, are fearful, dependent, hostile and unpredictable. Insecurely attached children find it difficult to explore their world and so have fewer opportunities to develop positive relationships with peers or teachers (Howes, Hamilton and Matheson, 1994; Dodge, Pettit and Bates, 1994). Researchers have identified gender differences between insecurely attached children, and insecurely attached girls were rated as more dependent and less assertive than securely attached girls (Turner, 1991).

Studies have found insecurely attached boys in comparison with securely attached children were:

- more aggressive;
- less well liked by peers;
- rated by teachers as less socially competent;
- more disruptive;
- more controlling. (Cohn, 1990; Turner, 1991)

In addition to attachment relationships, children's personalities influence how they adjust to family and classroom life and to people, events and situations. Teachers' personalities and children's personalities exert a mutual influence on classroom dynamics. Teachers might explain children's behaviour on the basis of particular personality characteristics, which, at times, will imply that nothing could be done to change the child's behaviour 'because she's that sort of child', which leads to a great deal of helplessness.

Understanding the importance of children's relationships with their caregivers can help teachers to think in different ways about children's behaviours. Teachers should not feel helpless about the situation or sorry for the child. Finding excuses for the child's behaviour on the grounds that he/she has a poor attachment relationship will do nothing to help the child learn to behave appropriately at school.

Importantly, teachers should not assume that the child's attachment relationship means there is nothing the school can do to help the child. Exciting research has shown that warm and supportive teacher–child relationships can help buffer the child from some of the effects of poor relationships with his/her parent (Howes, 1997; Pianta, 1997). The implication is that schools must not give up on children or assume that nothing can be done for them.

Children expect *unconsciously* that the teacher–child relationship will be like the parent–child relationship. Children who have experienced nurturing and consistent parenting will approach the teacher as the source of warmth and support, which is likely to evoke a similar response in the teacher.

Similarly, children who have experienced harshness and inconsistency in their relationship will expect the same from the teacher.

The relationship dynamics are subtle and often not within the participants' conscious awareness. Does it surprise you that teachers are most sensitive to and most involved with children who are securely attached? The opposite is also true; teachers are least sensitive to children who are insecurely attached and they spend less time with these children (Howes and Hamilton, 1992). It is easy to infer that needy children may become more deprived in some classrooms, as teachers find it easier to back away from them rather than trying to build relationships.

Relationships between teacher and children are complex. Relationships begin to develop as soon as the group meets and events and interactions take place rapidly. Often it is hard for teachers to stand back from the classroom long enough to identify what is happening in their relationships because teachers are part of the system themselves. One starting point for teachers is to become aware at how children adapt their emotions, cognitions, and social behaviours as they adjust to various contexts. It is important to understand that children's behaviour occurs within the context of relationships between the child/family and school (Pianta and Walsh, 1996).

In the systems model, children are viewed as open systems that have interrelated parts and processes that become woven together. There is a constant process of co-action between the child and the context that influence children to adapt in increasingly diverse and complex modes (Pianta and Walsh, 1996). When children's behaviour is seen as the outcome of how they have adapted to their family or school, then attention can be focused on all aspects of the child as a developing and interactive system. Emotions, cognitions, social and interactive skills are linked rather than fragmented into separate areas of development.

Children develop as they adapt to contextual challenges but at the same time the context responds to the child's adaptation. The metaphor of weaving may help to clarify the concept of interactive and responsive contexts. The weaving together of different types of fibres make a texture and pattern that is much more than the sum of their parts and it is the same with children.

Labelling children as intelligent or aggressive becomes inadequate when they are viewed as systems (Pianta and Walsh, 1996). Before a child is labelled as aggressive, teachers should clarify how they define aggression and how they respond to it. Teachers may ignore aggressive behaviour, diffuse it or support it. Teachers may enter into a power struggle where their goal is to maintain authority, or they may abandon their power in their efforts to keep the peace. Children will adapt their cognitions, emotions and behaviours according to the emerging relationships within and between systems.

The idea that children adapt to the system is important because it is different from the notion of stimulus-response that is a key principle of the behavioural model. Children do more than respond behaviourally to positive reinforcement such as praise or rewards. Pianta and Walsh (1996, p. 103) cite Greenspan who suggests that children develop diverse modes and goals of adaptation, defined as follows:

Modes of adaptation:

These are the capacities and skills that the child uses to adapt to certain contextual challenges. Children experience contextual challenges when they attend any type of group setting. Being one of 25 children will never be the same as being at home with mum or dad. Similarly, children experience contextual challenges when they move from one class to the next and have to get used to a new teacher, new rules and new ways of succeeding. Children's modes of adaptation to transitions include the ways they use their capacities and skills to develop relationships with their teachers and peer group.

Goals of adaptation:

The child seeks a match between the contextual challenges and their cognitions. For example, the goal of children's adaptation to a new class will be to achieve a match between their cognitions and emotions about the context (which includes their expectations) that feel right. Therefore:

- being an isolate feels normal to a child with a history of being isolated;
- being a victim feels normal to a child with a history of being bullied;
- being a social star feels normal to a child with a history of love, attention and encouragement.

Teachers can gain insights into children's thinking that guides their adaptive behaviour by asking children to talk about what they know or feel about the classroom and their relationships within it. Children may struggle to express themselves and some children will be reluctant to open up to teachers unless trust relationships have been developed. However, it is worth spending time and effort helping children feel comfortable to talk about what they know.

It is important to remember that you will need to listen to children and accept their view of the world. You may see the situation very differently but what is true is not the issue at stake. Seeking to understand children's ways of adapting to contextual challenges could lead to practical ways to help children develop more appropriate classroom behaviours.

The following case documents a child's difficulties in the classroom and the purpose in relating it here is to help you understand how relationships have histories that shape the present. Teachers have no capacity to change history, but understanding relationship dynamics can help teachers take different action regarding a child with troublesome behaviours. As you read through this case try and relate the material to any child you have known who has triggered similar feelings of surprise or confusion in you.

Jake – A child with insecure relationships

Beth Lee was aware that different children sparked different responses in her and sometimes she was puzzled by the strength of her feelings. She found Jake a particularly difficult child from the beginning of the school year and told her colleague, 'There's just something about him that gets to me. I don't know what it is, I just feel uncomfortable around him'.

Within the first few weeks of school Beth realised that other children were shrinking away from Jake, who was a stocky child with the loudest voice in the class. Beth told staff that Jake was dynamite: perpetual motion of the most destructive kind. His pathway from the door to his seat provided many opportunities for him to create chaos out of order. Staff laughed when Beth told them Jake's name. The family had quite a reputation and colleagues were quick to tell stories of disaster with Jake's older sibling. 'Your only hope is the red card', they told her. The red card was part of the school-based behaviour management system whereby perpetual troublemakers were withdrawn from class to a special room.

The school has a file on the family, which showed that his mother had neglected Jake. Jake's mother was not heartless and uncaring. She had been neglected as a child and lacked confidence in her parenting skills. She found herself living in poor housing with little money and no partner to support her in the job of parenting. Jake's mother loved her children but felt overwhelmed by their needs and had few resources to support her.

Knowing about Jake's family did nothing to help Beth and if anything, it made her feel more depressed as she wondered if there was anything that would make a difference to this child. Her worst fears were confirmed. Jake followed few of her instructions and showed no inclination to learn anything. His frequent outbursts of temper disrupted teaching and intimidated the other children. Soon Beth realised that most of her interactions with Jake were negative. She felt he was watching her constantly and deliberately baiting her at every possible opportunity. His eyes followed her around the room but he was unresponsive when she did initiate contact with him. Beth realised that she was avoiding contact with Jake and noticed that the children also kept their distance from him.

Beth remembered the principles of behaviour management she had learnt at university; giving children attention for their unwanted behaviour reinforced it. She decided to ignore as much of Jake's poor behaviour as possible. But this strategy resulted in a sudden rise in Jake's disruptive behaviour that led to some acts of aggression. Beth felt bewildered and at a loss to know how to help Jake. She found herself responding to Jake with increasing degrees of hostility.

Beth worked out that Jake engaged in deliberate acts of defiance. As a result, she gave him choices about his behaviour to help him accept the consequences. At times Beth talked to Jake about his behaviour and tried to help him understand how it affected his peers. However, Jake's troublesome behaviours increased yet again.

Beth found that talking to Jake did not alter his behaviour and she used the red card more often, which meant that she had an hour of peace while Jake was out of the room.

Beth felt unhappy about the situation. She found herself feeling on edge and flustered by Jake. She began to doubt her ability to manage this child or any other child who challenged her authority. She confided to a colleague, 'I get confused around Jake and doubt myself, then I either get tough on him or ignore him'.

All relationships have histories, and at times, Beth reacted to Jake from her personal history. Many teachers experience situations where their past shapes their present perceptions. Talking to a trusted professional could help Beth be clear about the past so that she could clarify her view of Jake. A relationship-based view of Jake's difficulties could guide Beth's plans to help Jake.

The way Jake behaved reflected the two-way flow of interactions between Jake and the context. Let us analyse some aspects of Jake's behaviour that puzzled Beth and make some inferences to explain Jake's behaviour:

1 *Why did Jake's troublesome behaviour escalate when Beth decided to ignore minor acts?*

Jake may have felt rejected when Beth ignored his uncompliant behaviour. Jake's aggressive 'macho man' front made it hard for Beth to see him as a troubled and scared boy who had no mental representations of how to get the support he needed to deal with the stress he experienced at school.

Jake's knowledge of relationships was based on his experiences of unpredictable care. Jake had to fight for attention (his mode of adaptation), but was scared when he got it because it could be withdrawn at any time, leaving him more vulnerable than before.

Jake struggled with his unconscious fears that his mother would abandon him, and the classroom situation reproduced these fears. Jake needed to engage with adults to ensure that they did not abandon him (his goal of adaptation), as when Beth ignored him then he felt rejected again. He dealt with this threat to his well being in the best way he knew, which was by increasing his demands for attention. He needed comfort and reassurance through psychological and physical closeness to his teacher, but the only way he knew how to get attention resulted in his teacher rejecting and isolating him.

Jake did not know how to regulate his emotions and did not know that a relationship with his teacher could be a resource to help him manage the school context. Jake needed proximity to Beth to help him deal with his stress but his behaviour ensured that she kept her distance. By distancing herself from Jake, Beth was not able to praise and encourage him for the good things that he did during the day. At the same time, Jake's peers imitated their teacher's model and either ignored Jake or rejected him by not including him in games and activities.

2 *Beth decided Jake was being manipulative rather than impulsive. She worked out that he had control over his behaviour and therefore she began to give him choices about how to behave and to explain to him about the consequences of his choices. But why did this lead to a sharp increase in his uncompliant acts?*
Jake's stress increased when Beth gave him choices, or engaged in lengthy discussions because they added to his cognitive load and he did not have the resources to deal with them. Jake needed his teacher to respond to him with clear limits that helped him define his boundaries and show him how to behave successfully.

3 *The school's policy was to isolate children who disrupted the classroom. However, time-out did not decrease Jake's troublesome behaviour. Why not?*
The school's policy meant that Jake was isolated in a room away from the classroom. Being isolated added to Jake's sense of alienation and heightened his fear of being abandoned. Jake was one child in the class with an urgent need to experience positive relationships but the red card system and class withdrawal meant that Jake missed opportunities to develop sustaining relationships with his teacher and peers. Jake had no mental images to label or regulate his frightening emotions, and being left alone deprived him of talking to anybody about his experiences.

Punitive strategies, such as isolating the child, are associated with accelerated levels of aggression and violence (Van Acker and Talbott, 1999). Reacting to behaviour with punishment does little to help children learn new ways of managing in the context (Tulley and Chiu, 1998).

Many unconscious motivations are driving Jake's behaviour, but he had the same basic needs as all children. The need to:

- belong to the group;
- rely on responsive adults;
- gain attention;
- have physical and psychological closeness to others;
- be valued by others;
- be respected for his ideas, knowledge, skills and imagination.

Jake's needs could be met in the context of his relationship with his teacher and peers that allowed him to count on:

- predictable and logical responses to his disruptive behaviour;
- teacher actions that were calm, clear and fair;
- the teacher's physical proximity;
- predictable routines;
- well-timed interventions.

Beth could begin to reshape her relationship with Jake by making her interactions with him *contingent on* his experiences, views, feelings and ideas. Making her interactions contingent on Jake's experiences means noticing what Jake was doing, listening to what he was saying and interpreting how he was feeling, and using those elements as the source of conversations. Beth's use of contingent interactions would convey to Jake that he was important in the world and she was interested in him. Beth needed to notice Jake when he was being compliant and then she should make a point of sitting with him and having a chat about what he was doing.

Through contingent interactions Beth would:

- listen and respond to Jake's view of the world;
- show respect for his life experiences;
- respond to his ideas and help him build on them;
- help Jake recognise and name his feelings;
- help Jake manage his anger; for example, recognising difficult situations, naming the feeling and seeking help from an adult.

Jake's case highlights the importance of seeing children's behaviour in context rather than as belonging to the individual, or resulting from individual deficits. Looking at relationships as a context for children's troublesome behaviours can help teachers to avoid feeling helpless in the face of classroom difficulties (Watkins and Wagner, 2000).

Jake's competencies as a learner would be nurtured when his teacher planned learning experiences that emerged from contingent interactions. A secure relationship with the teacher could provide Jake with a context to develop positive relationships with his peers by reducing his sense of isolation and rejection.

Fostering good relationships

Teachers who want to develop good relationships in the classroom must be able to model fairness, honesty, consideration and kindness (Charles, 2000). They must portray a sense of personal dignity and at the same time, demonstrate respect to all the children in the class. Teachers threaten trust relationships when they are indifferent or disrespectful to children (Charles, 2000). There are many strategies that teachers use to develop good learning relationships. The following section outlines two strategies that require teachers to listen to children and show interest in them; these are elements that foster trust and respect.

Contingent interactions

Using contingent interactions is one practical strategy that can help teachers develop sustaining relationships with all children. The educators in Reggio Emilia explain the idea as 'catching the children's ball and throwing it back' (Edwards, 1993, p. 153). Teachers who make their interactions contingent on the children's ideas, emotions, thoughts and knowledge are using a technique that is compatible with the principles of active learning.

Teachers who show interest in the child's world are able to build on children's competencies, strengths and motivations as learners. These teachers are prepared to balance their teaching goals with the child's agenda and use the information that results from contingent interactions to inform the planning of routine times, timetable, teaching strategies and curriculum content.

When teachers use contingent interactions they become a partner in the child's learning. They:

- look closely and notice what the child is doing;
- listen carefully and notice what the child is saying;
- follow the child's lead and respond to it;
- provide opportunities for all children to interact with their peers.

One way of beginning the process is for teachers to sit alongside a child and talk aloud in a soft and encouraging voice to describe what they see happening as the child interacts with materials or a peer. Often the child will do or say something to confirm or correct the teacher's musings and a conversation about the child's learning activity can take place.

When teachers use contingent interactions they:

- refrain from asking questions or talking to fill in the gaps;
- describe what they see the child or children doing, 'Mmmm your bridge is spanning two chairs and you've built it by making supports with the long blocks and struts with cardboard' (pause);
- pause to allow children to contribute, correct or add to the teacher's statement;
- acknowledge children's non-verbal signals, which may be a smile, quick eye contact, small shrug or a sigh and interpret these signals but leaving space for children to correct the teacher's incorrect interpretation;
- keep the conversation going by picking up children's contributions (verbal or non-verbal) by 'wondering'. For example, having noticed that the child is testing the bridge by placing cars on it, the teacher says, 'I wonder if the bridge is strong enough to hold more than five cars ...' (pause).

Teachers find that as they talk aloud that children respond and add to the teacher's observations, which gives extra insights and information to guide the conversation.

The value of describing aloud children's activities includes the following points:

- children feel supported to continue their learning activities;
- children feel important because the teacher has shown interested in what they are doing: their ideas and their actions;
- the teacher provides a positive role model of acceptance that other children can imitate, which is particularly important when a child is struggling to find a place in the group.

Contingent interactions align well with active learning approaches. However, it is important for teachers to keep checking that the classroom is a fair and equitable context for all children. Children must be able to rely on a consistent and responsive environment where rules are few and well maintained, where harshness and bias are banned and where all children are constructed as powerful learners and valuable members of the classroom.

Contingent interactions can open up relationships with children and can play a part in relationships with parents. Teachers who spend time listening to and responding to parents' ideas, feelings and life experiences can help form relationships based on parity and respect. Teachers use contingent interactions to get to know parents as people; show that they understand that parents and teachers are partners in the child's learning. When parents and teachers work as partners then teachers feel no pressure to educate parents into the way of the school and they are able to see the parent as a valuable resource.

Writing about concerns

Teachers use a variety of ways to develop relationships with individual children and encourage them to make their voice heard in the classroom. For example, in one classroom (Hail, 2000), children were encouraged to write notes on 'classroom concerns' to one another or to the teacher about things they like in the class, school, or things they would like to be changed. The notes were placed in a special 'classroom concern' envelope attached to a bulletin board and they were read first thing each morning.

The aim was to give children an opportunity to talk as a group about the positive and negative things that influenced the class. The teacher modelled note writing to the children, often to recognise their achievements or efforts. Importantly, the note writing spread to other teachers involved with the class and to the children's parents, which reinforced the positive classroom climate and trust relationships (Hail, 2000). In particular, relationships with parents changed when those who expected only to hear negative things about their child began to hear about notes celebrating achievements and contributions their child had made to the classroom (Hail, 2000).

Summary

This chapter has explored how new approaches to active learning makes a difference to how children behave in classrooms and why this may create difficulties for vulnerable children. Teachers may be able to help children adopt new behaviours for active learning when they work in the child's zone of proximal development by identifying what the child can do and what they need to do next to achieve success.

The chapter explained that relationships influence behaviours, and that teachers need to put considerable time and effort into developing positive relationships with all the children in the class. Teachers need to persevere, be determined and work hard, in order to develop good learning relationships with some children. Strategies, such as contingent interactions, are valuable in helping to change relationships with children, but there are no quick fixes. Teachers will have to be content with small steps forward and accept that there will be backward steps at times.

Teachers will need support through the bad days and they will need colleagues with whom they can let off steam and brainstorm ideas. Teachers need to be reassured of their professional expertise and reminded of the progress that is being made.

Adopting a relationship-based view of classrooms helps teachers provide a model of a supportive and sustaining relationships that enables all children to enjoy life in schools. Relationships can help teachers and parents together, to find ways to build on each child's competencies as a motivated learner, a collaborative peer and a good friend.

Chapter 3

Teachers and troublesome behaviour

> Some children don't have the staying power, their concentration drifts and they get into trouble.
>
> (Primary school teacher)

In this chapter I discuss what teachers know about children's troublesome behaviours and how it underpins their moment-by-moment decisions. An example of teacher's knowledge is seen in the extract at the top of this page, where the teacher says that children's troublesome behaviour is due to their lack of 'staying power'. This teacher would be likely to look at making changes to an individual child's behaviour rather than examining the curriculum content, teaching strategies, or learning relationships.

As you read this chapter, try to keep asking yourself how what you know shapes your actions. Have you ever found yourself in an unexpected situation with a child and reacted spontaneously in a particular way? Did you wonder later why you behaved like that? In those unexpected moment you act from intuition – hunches that come from your implicit store of knowledge. This chapter will help you understand more about your implicit knowledge and how it influences what you do.

Why is teachers' knowledge important in this book about troublesome behaviours? Many experts have suggested that teachers find children's behaviour difficult because they lack the skills to manage classrooms. It has been said that teachers are deficient in skills and should be 'improved'. You may believe that if you had better skills then children's troublesome behaviours would end, but this assumes that skills are the essential element in classroom management and that teachers will use skills that they are taught (Corrie, 1997). There are problems with this view because it ignores teachers' knowledge, which is shaped by the school context in which they work.

What you know is influenced by your personal and professional values and beliefs, as well as teacher education and professional development courses. The school context, the principal and teaching colleagues influence what you know and do in your classroom. Knowledge is not fixed and you are likely to change, update and delete knowledge as you experience dynamic relationships with your teaching colleagues, the children, and their families.

Knowing about children's behaviour

Many things happen quickly in classrooms and events occur together. Teachers don't have the luxury of attending to only one child or event at a time. Teachers act from the intuition because the swift pace of many situations gives them little time to reflect and plan ahead.

Intuition is the 'gut feeling' that teachers have about their classrooms and it's not something that they spend time talking about. Teachers have intuitions about children, about teaching and learning, what makes classrooms tick and what schools in a particular town or suburb need to do to get along with families and the community.

Teachers' intuitions guide their practice, which includes the ways in which they deal with children's behaviour. However, in our information-laden lives we hold many bits of knowledge at an implicit or intuitive level. We 'just know' certain things and we don't stop to think about it or talk to others about what we know or how we know it. Teachers often talk about their 'gut feelings', for example, when one teacher spoke about assessing children she explained, 'Things are often intangible ... you can't state what they are, but you just have a feeling about a child'. Another teacher said: 'A lot of my knowledge is based on hunches ... it's on knowing the children' (Corrie, 1999, p. 40).

Many teachers accept that their hunches shape what they do and they don't often talk or write about them or make them *explicit*. Teachers act on their feelings and hunches many times during a busy school day, and their intuition guides them in many different ways.

Acting intuitively means that we do not have to think through the reasons for our actions and it is hard for us to explain the reasons for them to other people, which can cause problems when teachers are required to be accountable for their decisions. However, talking with colleagues about a child's troublesome behaviour offers teachers help in many ways. First, letting off steam about a child is an important outlet for a teacher's strong feelings and can provide a valuable and therapeutic release from tension. Second, when teachers talk to one another about a child, or particular troublesome behaviours, they have an opportunity to put their intuitions into words and get to know more about the ideas that shape their views of children.

The way teachers see children is influenced by:

- memory;
- expectations;

- perceptions;
- motivations.

Talking can help teachers make their knowledge explicit. What teachers know is not vague 'pie in the sky', but it is the unseen force that influences their actions in many ways, for example, how they:

- respond to troublesome behaviour;
- develop relationships with children and their families;
- plan the curriculum;
- use resources;
- select teaching strategies;
- manage their classrooms.

Teachers' knowledge contributes to their theories that they use to explain events, relationships and difficulties they experience in classrooms. As the opening extract shows, teachers may talk about children's behaviour as if it is solely the responsibility of the individual child. One flaw in this view is that it directs attention *away from* the context where the behaviour occurs. Changing children's behaviour to fit the context, without first examining the context can lead to injustice.

An example of how teachers' knowledge leads them to develop theories to explain behaviour was seen when one teacher described the parents of the children he taught as being from 'very mixed ethnic backgrounds' from the lower socio-economic group who had little contact with the school. At the same time the teacher said that one child's troublesome classroom behaviour was due to his mother because:

> She is often in such a state. He comes to school late. He comes to school very over-excited. There is very little organisation at home, and very little routine. Now he comes to school and the situation is based around routine and rules and so on, ... and he finds it very difficult to cope with that freedom and what he's allowed to do and what he's not allowed to do, because of course at home he's allowed to do almost anything.

The teacher inferred a great deal from brief and infrequent interactions with the boy's mother, for example, that she was not organised and she allowed her son too much freedom. The teacher used inferences to deduce reasons for the boy's responses to the classroom. The teacher talked as if he *knew* what went on at home but he had few facts about the boy's life outside the school. What the teacher knew about the family had been constructed from what he perceived and expected from 'this sort of family', which could be right or wrong.

Staff may make judgements about children's families that are based on their own values. Personal values then underpin suppositions that guide the teacher's actions. Examples of personal values are seen in statements such as:

- 'She's from a broken family you know';
- 'The dad's unemployed again and the mum is expecting her fifth – hopeless';
- 'They're strict Muslims (fundamental Christians, new age, Buddhists) and you know what that means';
- 'She's a typical Italian (middle Eastern, Indian, Japanese) mother and everybody knows they spoil their sons rotten'.

Talking to others can help teachers understand that their personal values are embedded in what they know. Personal values cannot be separated from teachers' interactions with the children or the decisions they take in a split second that encompass the words they use, tone of voice, proximity to the child, body posture and facial expressions. When teachers work alone in classrooms without the opportunity to collaborate with colleagues then much of their knowledge is not available for them to reflect on or change.

Alongside judgements about children's families, social justice might be transgressed when teachers construct troublesome classroom behaviours as belonging to individuals rather than the whole classroom context. The teacher who assumes that troublesome behaviour belongs to the individual does not investigate the classroom context that is the setting for the behaviour and does not question other children's roles, or the classroom rules and practices that may influence behaviour.

Teachers get to know about children as they work with them, and they gain additional knowledge from their interactions with families, school records, and teachers' assessments. What difference does it make whether the teacher thinks one way or another about the child's family? It makes a difference because the teacher's knowledge influences what he/she does. It is likely that some of the teacher's knowledge comes from his judgements about 'this sort of family', which may be quite different from inferences that he might make if the children were from white, middle-class origins.

Everybody makes assumptions and inferences when there is little factual knowledge and teachers are no exception. However, there is a danger that teachers' knowledge might be shaped by bias, which remains hidden when teachers do not have opportunities to talk seriously about what they know. Teachers' expectations are shaped by their knowledge of children's:

- gender;
- race;
- ethnicity;

- family structure;
- education of parents;
- and socio-economic group.

Teachers' expectations may be influenced by their own personal histories, socio-economic background, ethnicity or race, and family experiences. Teachers develop ideas that enable them to give reasons for children's behaviour, which is seen in the following extract when a teacher explained that he treated children as individuals because he knew their families, and that many children in his class lived in challenging situations:

> ... one (child) is in a very very bad situation, which has actually been going on for a very long time, and he is from a family that split up a long time ago. His father went to live with his male lover, and now his male lover has died of AIDS, and the father has actually gone back into the circle of the family but he's not living with them, though they are closer than they were. And in that situation obviously this little boy has had to grow up and learn lots of things which he wouldn't have learned at first hand about at such a young age. This has been going on since he was about five or six, and he's now nine, and as a result, his behaviour is highly erratic.

The teacher's ideas about the boy were shaped by what he knew about the family, which influenced how he managed the child's behaviour. The teacher showed sensitivity towards the child and had decided that when the boy was having a hard day he would be asked to have some time alone so that he did not disturb the classroom. The boy's time alone was not punishment for misdemeanours but some cooling-down time.

The facts themselves – that the boy's father left the family and then returned – was similar to several other children in the class, and other children did not get special treatment from the teacher. It was the teacher's construction of the meanings about the father's male lover and his death from AIDS that led him to particular understandings of the boy's disruptive behaviour. As a result of the teacher's ideas, he decided to go easy on the boy and not challenge his troublesome behaviour. Would the teacher have made different decisions if his understandings of the circumstances had been different? For example, the teacher might have made a different decision about the boy's behaviour if the father had gone to live with a female partner.

Were the teacher's actions helping the boy? Classroom observations showed that the boy was unpredictable and aggressive and that he spent a large percentage of his day outside the room. The teacher said there had been little change in the boy's behaviour, which is what the school expected in the circumstances. Removing the boy from the room preserved some semblance of order and allowed teaching and learning to progress. The teacher's response to the child was consistent, which allowed him to maintain an equitable relationship with the child, but overall, little positive change took place over the year.

Imagine that you are the boy's teacher, what would you do? How would you deal with this child? You may think the teacher's approach is the best one, in which case try to clarify your reasons.

Think about a child you've known whose behaviour has caused you concern, possibly a child who came from a challenging family. Write down the practical steps you took to manage the behaviour.

Once you have some ideas written down, try to think through your reasons for your management strategies. Do they reflect the way you see the child and the situation.

How do your personal values about this type of situation influence how you would manage the situation?

Sharing your views with a colleague would be useful.

The teacher's actions could be interpreted in many different ways. One view might say that the teacher is a pragmatist who wasn't prepared to hit his head against a brick wall. Another person might say that the teacher's ideas about the child's family life were linked to his personal values and led to feelings of helplessness. Helplessness, believing that nothing would make a difference, resulted in a passive approach to the problem. The teacher did not actually help the child learn new ways to behave but he had found a way for the class to survive the year.

It would be useful for you to spend some time thinking about the class you teach or know. Start with one or two children who stand out in your mind and begin to get aware of how you think about them.

What do you expect from these children and how do your inner values shape your expectations?

How fair and just is it that your personal values shape judgements about the children?

Have you clarified your personal values recently? Try writing a list that represents the five most important values.

Teachers expect different behaviours from children, based on their understandings of their needs, this was expressed by one teacher as follows:

> They don't need rules up – they all know and remember the rules. But it depends on each individual child – I can't say there's one way. Josh will mess around unless he's doing something, I've noticed that, if he is doing something that he really enjoys he'll do it all day, and he doesn't mind doing it all day, and he won't disturb anyone, and he's great.

Look carefully at the extract and you will see several contradictory ideas about rules and establishing appropriate behaviour. For example:

1 Children know how to behave therefore they don't need rules contradicts the idea that rules are not necessary because classroom management is tailored for each individual child.
2 Children remember how to behave contradicts the view that a child doesn't behave unless he's doing something he enjoys.

I am highlighting the contradictions in order to emphasise that classroom management is complex and that teachers make decisions quickly as they weigh up a range of different factors. Teachers may have contradictory ideas, but they are unaware of them because they don't talk to others about what they know and the contradictions remain hidden. It probably won't surprise you to know that Josh's teacher worked in a school where the staff group was fragmented. Teachers seldom talked to others about the troublesome behaviours that faced them each day and the senior management team provided no opportunities for staff to reflect on difficulties or problem-solve together.

Teachers bring their knowledge of the family/home contexts to bear on their decisions about children in the classroom on a particular day. Meanings are negotiated, so that the teacher accepts Josh's behaviour even though others might not. The relationships within the context allow members to interact, make sense, have their place, and continue to negotiate meanings that enable the class to work. However, teachers often work in isolation and at times their intuitions about a child may be faulty and divert them from achieving their goals for the child or the class.

What teachers know, social justice and children's behaviour

Injustice can be enacted in many ways in the classroom. For example, injustice can occur when teachers assume information about a child without collecting objective information. It is likely that some of the teacher's knowledge comes from his judgements about 'this sort of family', which may be quite different from inferences that he might make if the children were from white, middle-class origins.

When teachers are aware of children's extenuating home circumstances then they may feel helpless because they know that they can do little to change the child's family. Helplessness leads teachers to lower their expectations for some children, particularly those from:

- minority groups;
- children from different family structures;
- children from low socio-economic groups.

It is true that understanding elements of units in a system will change nothing about an individual's behaviour but it may lead to changes in what teachers know and do in the classroom. As you read the following case, try to identify what the teacher knows about children's behaviour and how it is directing her actions.

> Bad news travels fast in a small country town and I heard about Robert before he stepped foot inside the classroom. People were keen to tell me about Robert's experiences in his 'broken' family, his bad behaviour and his aggressive ways. I decided I must keep an open mind as labelling children doesn't help them and neither does pity. We needed to get to know Robert by forming a trust relationship with him and by observing him in our context, which is my aim for all the children. We decided that if there were difficulties we would investigate them objectively ...
>
> Several weeks later I realised that I felt drained by sorting out incidents concerning Robert. I looked through his file and saw anecdotal records documenting a string of incidents. His troublesome behaviour was escalating. Obviously some elements of the classroom weren't working for him and we needed to change ...
>
> (Corrie, Chadbourne and Maloney, 1998)

What did this teacher know about children and what was guiding her? She did not blame the child for his behaviour, and did not become helpless by blaming his family background. Her reasoning can be interpreted like this:

- 'I decided I must keep an open mind ...'
  She did not pay attention to gossip or come to quick judgements based on bias.
- 'We need to get to know Robert ...'
  She believed that getting to know the child was essential and that relationships were important in the teaching and learning situation.
- 'Obviously some elements of the classroom weren't working for him ...'
  When she reflected on Robert's behaviour she did not blame the child but realised that she needed to think about the classroom context.
- '... and we needed to change'
  She believed that children can be helped to enact appropriate behaviour when changes are made to the context rather than deciding the child needed to change his behaviour.

The teacher held certain knowledge that shaped her perceptions of Robert's behaviour, and this knowledge led her to think about how she can help the child. It is not hard to infer that this teacher's knowledge would lead her to develop a supportive relationship with the child with troublesome behaviours.

Contrast the story of Robert with the following story about William and as you read, try and identify how injustice may be occurring:

> At the age of seven, William was withdrawn from school and placed in a special unit for children with behaviour disorders because he had created problems in class by often passively resisting the teacher's instructions. William was an only child and his bicultural parents (Chinese mother and English father) worked for long hours leaving William alone to fend for himself. His parents were described as loving but unaware of the emotional and social needs of a young child as constructed in the society where they lived. After a year in the special unit William made good progress and was integrated back into a primary school.
>
> His new teacher was nervous about taking a child from the special unit but agreed. However, a few weeks later the support unit got an emergency call when it was reported that William had violent temper tantrums and had destroyed school property. Teachers at the unit were puzzled, as William was never known to be aggressive or destructive. He could be very 'obstinate' and 'dig his heels in' but was not an acting out type of child.
>
> The teacher who had worked closely with William went to the school, and spoke first to William. He was silent and remote at first and seemed mortified that his 'old' teacher had been called to the school. After some time, he opened up and shared that since he arrived at his new school he had been teased regularly about being one of the bad kids from the unit. Kids had snatched his lunch and his cap was used as a football. He found it hard to join games and said nobody wanted to play with him or be his friend. William had dealt with the situation by withdrawing, becoming silent and bottling up his feelings until another lunchtime when he was teased again as he entered the classroom. He said 'I didn't control myself' and with tears in his eyes described how he picked up a school pencil and broke it in two, and then had pushed a book off his desk.
>
> William's teacher repeated her claim about violence and destruction, but when pressed for specific detail could not add more to William's story. It seems that the teacher judged breaking a pencil and pushing a book off a desk as a violent temper tantrum, although the staff of the unit rated it at about 1 on the temper tantrum scale of 1 to 10! The teacher did not know about the teasing and bullying William had tolerated until his breaking point but hinted that if William was going to continue to cause trouble he would have to be removed from the school.

Had William experienced social justice? It seems that judgements made about him on the basis of the teacher's fears and fantasies rather than factual evidence. The teacher had not documented objective evidence of William's behaviour, and preferred to rely on her subjective opinions. The teacher had relied on her impression of William, the special unit he came from and her knowledge about the 'type' of children that attended the unit. The school had taken no steps to develop a positive relationship with William, or enable him to develop good relationships with his peers. Instead, the children had been warned that William was one of the *naughty boys* who had been in a special unit, and the teacher responded to her perceptions of his deficits, which led her to judge that *this boy was trouble*.

The knowledge that William's teacher had constructed about him had been shaped by prejudice and stereotyping, and these attributes had influenced his relationships with his peers. It seemed that the teacher had not been able to develop a relationship with William that may have helped her see beyond her stereotype of this 'naughty boy'. William's story shows us how teachers' judgements may be influenced by their knowledge about children's histories, family backgrounds and experiences.

Teachers have a professional responsibility to make objective assessment of children's progress in the interests of social justice. However, applying the systems model to the story of William, we have to ask what support the school had given the teacher who was expected to integrate William into her class. For example:

- had the school made any provision for the teacher to have time to get to know William as an individual or in a small group of learners?
- had the school allowed the teacher time to assess William's social and educational competencies?
- had the principal or senior staff made provision to give support of any type to the staff group?

The school might have organised for some team-teaching or support staff to enable the teacher to develop positive relationships. In addition, the school might have arranged for a senior teacher to liaise with the classroom teacher to ensure that William's integration was running smoothly or to talk over any emerging problems. In fact, the teacher had received no support because the school was not able to fund it and neither was the special unit that had organised William's integration, due to budget cuts at the system level.

Investigating William's troublesome behaviour meant identifying the definitions of troublesome behaviour used by the teacher and the class, and the strategies used to help William. In addition it meant looking at how William's behaviour had contributed to his exclusion from the class and isolation from his peers.

You may find it helpful to talk about or write about the case of William in order to identify your views about social justice and individual children. Do you agree that William's case is an example of injustice? Try and explain specifically elements you feel strongly about.

You may find it helpful to write a brief case study of a child you know in order to tease out how hidden factors of relationships between units of the system might have influenced your thinking and decision making about a child with troublesome classroom behaviour.

In asking you to think and talk about social justice and William, I do not want to imply that children do not misbehave, or that teachers should 'excuse' troublesome behaviour. William, like many children, did exhibit challenging behaviours. The behaviour of children often causes teachers a great deal of stress and anxiety, and many teachers are surprised by children's responses that seem unreasonable and illogical. However, teachers may perceive behaviour in terms of individual deficit and blame the child, which suggests that *it's their fault*, that leads so easily to *and there is nothing I can do about it*. As I discuss in the following section, teachers' knowledge forms the theories that they use to explain children's behaviour.

Teachers' theories about children and learning

All teachers have theories to explain children's behaviours. Theories are simply the systems of ideas that people hold to account for events, behaviours, successes and failures. Theories are shaped by particular perspectives and experiences, so that if your favourite football team was thrashed your theory may be that:

- the coach ran out of steam;
- the best player was off-colour;
- the umpire was biased;
- the opposition took steroids.

A supporter of the winning team however, probably theorises that they won because they were better football players, they trained hard and they were hungry for a win. Of course, the two theories to explain the success or failure are shaped by the perspective of the person.

Theories don't belong to academics in universities. Every person has theories to help them understand events in their daily life. Teachers' theories about children, families, learning and development, and their own roles as teachers shape how they perceive and think about children's behaviour. What you know about children has been shaped by history, by past ideas as well as by current views. In the course of reading the following section, I hope you will take the time to explore your own theories about children's behaviour. Often teachers are surprised by their feelings when they begin to explore the origins of their theories.

A beginning point is to think about your own experiences as a child in school, and some of the significant events that stand out for you. The life experiences may be big events or they may be brief interactions with others that you have never forgotten. An example is seen in Stuart's story:

> I had terrible writing when I was seven and one day my teacher gave me a pencil covered with silver foil. She told me it was a magic pencil that would help me learn to write neatly. I didn't really buy the magic story but remember an excited tingle of hope.
>
> Like any curious child, the first thing I did (when the teacher wasn't looking) was to rip off the foil and find out the truth about the pencil. I discovered it was just an ordinary 'beginners' pencil. The other kids in my class teased me about having to use it. I've never forgotten how humiliated, disappointed and different I felt, and I knew I wasn't as good as the others and would never be like them. Needless to say I quickly lost the pencil, my writing didn't improve at all and I became the class troublemaker. Now I realise that I lost my belief in myself as a learner and trust in the teacher.
>
> Children learn when they are treated with respect, and teachers have the responsibility to talk to them honestly about their skills and what they need to learn. Children need to be included in plans, and above all, need to believe in their capacities as learners.

Stuart's story is about feeling different and abnormal, and the influence it had on his motivation to learn and ideas of self-efficacy. His theory is about respect, honesty and children's images of themselves shaping the process of learning.

> You may find it helps to talk or write about your personal experiences that may have shaped your ideas and theories of teaching. Triumphs and disappointments may be deep in our memories but have influenced what we know in powerful and covert ways.
>
> Talking about personal experiences may help you to recognise your own systems of ideas that form your theories.
>
> Clarifying your personal theories may help you to understand why you react in a particular way to a certain child or a certain type of behaviour.

The following section reports a study that investigated the theories and practice of four teachers. I am sharing these teachers' stories with you to encourage you to think carefully about your own theories of teaching and learning. As you read try to relate the material to yourself and your experiences in classrooms as this will help you begin to make your implicit knowledge clear to you.

Findings of the study showed that each teacher's theory influenced the way they managed their classrooms, at times, without them knowing about it. The teachers were invited to participate in the study because they said they aimed to empower children as learners. This position aligned well with the active learning approaches that were being promoted in the teachers' four schools, and the focus was the type of learning behaviours discussed in Chapter 2.

The researcher (Moore, 1999) was interested to find out what the teachers meant by 'empowering children' and how they went about it. This meant knowing how the teachers organised their classrooms and curriculum, and how they guided children's behaviour.

Empowering children

This study included two teachers who taught in classrooms in the United Kingdom and two who taught in Australia. A collective case study was constructed by observing teachers and children in the classroom, making field notes, filming with a video camera, talking with teachers and collecting documents such as teachers' philosophies, children's work samples, and classroom time-tables.

Some of the videotapes were used as part of research strategy called 'stimulated recall'. Stimulated recall is a useful strategy that can be used by teaching colleagues who want to foster positive practice. In this study, teachers were shown parts of the videos in private interviews to help them recall specific incidents and talk about why they acted in a particular way. For example, the researcher might show a segment and then say, 'I noticed that in the segment when a child asked you where the drawing paper was, you asked her to think about it. Please talk about your reasons for saying this'. If the video showed a teacher intervening firmly with a child, they would be asked to talk about their reasons for the action, and to talk about what they were thinking at that time.

Findings showed that the four teachers (Christine, Hannah, Pamela and Ellen) knew different things about empowering children as learners, these were demonstrated in different practices. For example, the teachers gave varying weight to their ideas about children's self-worth, and their capacities to form opinions, collaborate, and negotiate, and these different interpretations could be seen in their daily practice, which is discussed in the following section.

Christine

Christine saw her main teaching role as helping children to progress through levels of development by setting up the environment and allowing children to explore it. Christine emphasised the importance of encouraging children to develop independence. For example, when talking about how children tackled learning tasks she said that she wanted children to:

> Work it out themselves (so that) they don't need me next time.

Christine's emphasis on independence reflected her knowledge about how children learn. She did not believe that teachers should give children facts or information because she maintained that children did not learn from being told and usually the teacher had to:

> ... tell them again and again and again ... They are relying on me and I don't want that. I want them, even if there is a problem they don't know, (to try) it themselves without running to me first.

Christine said that expecting children to select their own learning tasks was an important element of her approach, because:

> I like them to be able to go and choose and test themselves at their level (of development).

Christine's statement showed how she merged her knowledge about independence with her knowledge about their developmental levels. Christine implied that children know intuitively what level of development they had achieved, and that they progressed naturally to the next level in the hierarchy.

Christine's theory of learning reflected her theory of teaching, which included organising the environment so that it encouraged children to test themselves. The importance of children's independent actions was seen in many different areas of the programme when Christine taught children what to do and then stood back to allow them to practice their skills.

Christine's view of independence influenced the way she structured the weekly timetable to keep the class to a strict routine. Christine explained that keeping to a routine enabled children to be independent because they knew what was expected of them on the different days. Similarly, she maintained an orderly environment to allow children to access materials and equipment easily, which stimulated children to make their own decisions about their next learning task. Christine said that the materials and equipment helped children to select and 'test themselves' at their own level.

Christine stressed the importance of children selecting their own learning tasks, and consequently she allocated blocks of time in the weekly timetable for children to investigate materials and objects she had placed in the environment. Christine then used small group learning experiences to monitor children's learning achieved during their self-selected activities in order to see:

> ... if they have developed and learnt any skills or knowledge that we have been talking about ... and I can see different levels

Christine's knowledge about the importance of observing different developmental levels was seen in her choice of group time learning experiences, which included games that were played on particular days. These games were structured to allow Christine to gain information about the children's developmental level. For example, one game was a variation of musical chairs, and the children had to follow instructions about spatial concepts in order to play the game 'Find something to stand on top of'. Christine stopped the music and the children found a suitable object to be 'on top of', and Christine asked a child:

Christine: ... Jason, what are you on top of? (paused)
Jason: Don't know.
Christine: Look.
Christine: What are you on top of? ...
Look at what you're on top of. (paused)
Jason: Table.
Christine: No, you're not standing on a table.
Jason: A chair.
Christine: A chair!

Chistine said that this exchange allowed her to assess children's developmental level, and she explained:

> ... they have to articulate where they are, and then I know if there is someone and they've got no idea, I need to work with them.

Christine's use of questioning helped her identify children's needs and to monitor children's progress from one developmental level to another.

Christine's theory of teaching was seen in a small group learning experience when children were asked to draw a picture using the starter, *At the beach I like...which* was printed at the top of the piece of paper. The pictures were to be used to make a class book. Christine's idea that familiarity was important to children's learning experience had informed her planning of the learning task. Christine explained to the children, 'You've got to tell me a sentence', and her conversation with Jason showed how she managed the experience:

(Jason stood next to Christine as she held his completed picture on her lap)

Christine: Jason, beautiful. (looking at his picture) At the beach I like?
Jason: Um, I went, I went to swim in the sea.
Christine: No, listen to me (she pointed to each word). At the beach I like ... What do you like doing at the beach? (paused). What do you like doing at the beach?
Jason: Swim.
Christine: Good one, that finishes it off. I like to (looks at Jason)
Jason: Swim
Christine: Swim. Good boy. You know how to swim because you've been to swimming lessons. We just have to finish it off.
Jason: Under the water.
Christine: Well done ...

Christine explained that she wanted to give children experience in making a group book, and she wanted it to be:

> ... something familiar. I wanted them to give me, give me a sentence for a group book so that we could do a shared reading with their familiar experiences. So that they can see that what they can tell me can be written down as a sentence or a story that is related to them, to see if they have developed and learnt any skills or knowledge that we have been talking about ... And I can see different levels here, drawing (as she looks through the children's work samples) ... So it's a good model to see what stage they are at; their language etc. their fine muscle and their drawing skills.

Christine maintained that familiar experiences were empowering to children because they knew what to expect, which helped them to learn.

Commentary

Christine wanted to foster independence but she controlled children's behaviour in covert ways. For example, children were encouraged to select materials and equipment in the environment but there was no procedure for them to request other materials or follow their own interests in learning experiences that had not been planned by the teacher. Christine assumed she knew what children wanted to learn, but did not ask children as she believed that children 'naturally' move to the next developmental level.

Christine emphasised the importance of children's independence because she wanted them to test themselves, however she had to stay in control of the children's learning in order to assess their developmental progress. This knowledge led Christine to refuse to scribe Jason's original sentence of *I went to swim in the sea* and Jason had to comply with his teacher. Christine explained her decision by saying that she needed to keep to her planned structure in order to facilitate the child to reach the next level in the developmental hierarchy.

Christine's focus was on the cognitive development of each individual, which excluded the socio-cultural context in the classroom and how it might affect the children's learning. If we look at the teaching incidents from Jason's point of view, we may want to ask questions about Jason's feelings. How did Jason feel about being questioned in front of his peers? What did the children know about Jason? How did the teacher's technique shape Jason's views of himself as a learner, and his relationships with his teacher and peers?

You may consider how well Christine's theory about empowering learners fits with your own theory.

Your context will be different from Christine's but elements of Christine's story will apply to all teaching situations. For example, how do you manage situations when a child is not showing the competencies expected, and how do you keep track of children's progress when change is rapid and ongoing.

How did you respond to the swimming at the beach story? Try and put yourself into Jason's shoes. If you were Jason, how might you feel about yourself as a learner?

Hannah and Pamela

Christine's theory of empowering young learners was different from Hannah and Pamela's theories. Hannah was from the United Kingdom and Pamela from Australia.

The knowledge and practices of Hannah and Pamela showed that they were influenced by Vygotsky's (1934/1986) theory of learning, but their individual personal and professional experiences shaped their own theories of teaching and learning.

Hannah and Pamela's knowledge reflected elements of Vygotsky's theory that emphasised the importance of context in children's learning. According to Vygotsky, learning takes places as a social process and that children learn through their interactions with more knowledgeable others, these may be adults or peers. In Vygotsky's theory, 'scaffolding' is an important role for the teacher to enact. Scaffolding occurs when the teacher guides, models or cues higher order thinking processes in order to help the child internalise knowledge and concepts, which applies to classroom behaviour as well as academic tasks.

The influence of Vygotsky was seen in the teachers' explanations of their understanding and aims of empowering young learners. Empowerment as an important construct was highlighted in Pamela's programme philosophy where she stated:

> Learning opportunities to help children to develop as empowered learners are planned with an emphasis on active learning through play and discovery, individual choice, using the project approach to explore children's interests, and through extensive social interactions with peers, teachers and the environment (indoors and outdoors).

Pamela said she encouraged children 'to believe in themselves' in many ways. She wanted children to influence the learning environment, for example, she supported children to select their own topics of learning. Pamela believed that she empowered children by expecting them to talk about their special interests that they were encouraged to pursue.

Hannah's theory about empowerment linked the child and the teacher. She believed that the empowered children formed their own opinions, had a sense of their self-worth and felt they had ownership of their work. Hannah said that empowered children were able to problem-solve, reason and make decisions, which were important life-skills and added that in her classroom children were:

> ... given room to think and to articulate their thoughts, to make decisions for themselves, and at the simplest level, if there is something they need ... they can go and get it without saying 'I need a pair of scissors', or, 'I've dropped my pencil ...'

Hannah said that the teacher had to empower children. Hannah maintained that adult expectations had a powerful effect on children as empowered learners and described the type of behaviours that teachers expected:

> We expect them to respond, to care for equipment, to help each other, to put things away ... to negotiate, to share when they are doing activities.

Like Hannah, Pamela referred to the important life-skills that children were developing in the classroom. She explained that she expected children to make decisions and reasoned judgements, partly because children needed particular skills to support them:

> When they are older to be able to make decisions and judgements and say 'no' to peers that are trying to encourage them to do something that they know inside themselves ... isn't right. Just to have that strength, to be able to make their own decisions and stand up for those beliefs ...

Pamela believed that allowing children to make decisions in the classroom contributed to them developing valuable life skills.

Pamela said she saw the classroom context as providing a zone of proximal development for children, which allowed them to learn through their interactions with materials and equipment, as well as adults and peers. Consequently, Pamela aimed to organise an environment that responded to the learner. Equipment was stored to facilitate easy access and exploration; the curriculum emerged from their ideas or was negotiated with them, and their learning experiences were respected, valued, and integrated into the fabric of the classroom life through opportunities to share with others. Pamela's ideas about the environment were linked to her belief that children were:

> ... self determining. They know what they want to learn about, they know what their needs are themselves ... I think they are very capable, a lot more capable than a lot of people give them credit for. I think that because they are so curious and have that innate need to know and find out about things. We can structure environments to foster that, and that it is all too easy, and I think that it happens in too many schools, that we make decisions for them and we plan for them and organise for them, and they are capable of doing all these things themselves.

Like Pamela, Hannah emphasised that children were able, competent individuals, and she said that it was her responsibility to create opportunities to help them develop their skills and knowledge further. Hannah emphasised the importance of children's choices and she linked it to the way she had set up the classroom:

> We set out as much equipment as possible, and children can access it when they need it. So if they are at a technology type table and they are cutting and sticking and so on I do not get out things like scissors for them, they go and get their own scissors and bring them back and use them and put them away again.

Hannah's statement shows that her decisions about organising the environment and her expectations of children's behaviour are informed by her knowledge that children are competent and able.

The idea that children are capable of making choices and decisions was linked to Hannah's view of independence. Hannah linked independence with security. She said that classroom routines gave children a feeling of security but at the same time the children knew that they were free to explore and make decisions about their learning experiences. Hannah sought to help children grow as empowered learners by balancing:

- routine with innovative activities;
- security with independence;
- child-initiated and teacher-directed learning.

Routines in Pamela's class were constructed to help children experience a feeling of belonging to the group, which was linked to the Vygotskian principal that learning is a social activity. For example, when children arrived at the class in the morning they 'self-registered' by finding their name card and placing it in a box. Pamela said:

> They get to know their friend's name and who is here and they will often come and say to me, 'Kelly isn't here today', ... and it is just that feeling of, 'I'm here and I'm part of this group'.

Like Pamela, Hannah emphasised the importance of peer interaction and small group interactive learning, which reflected her knowledge that children learnt by constructing their own knowledge. Hannah sought to balance child-initiated learning and teacher-directed learning. She identified certain learning outcomes that she hoped children would achieve and she structured certain learning experiences around them. She did not give a choice about certain learning experiences because she wanted all children to participate, but she thought that they:

> ... should know why they are doing it because how can they really learn unless they know?

As a result of Hannah's theory of learning, she emphasised the importance of planning time when she explained to children what they were expected to participate in during the day, and from which activities they could choose. Hannah emphasised that planning time fostered a sense of security in the children and empowered them as learners. She said that scaffolding was central to her teaching role, which she demonstrated by asking the children particular questions or offering suggestions when they were faced with problems, without telling children what to do:

> I feel that our skill as a teacher ... comes (from) knowing when to intercede, when to ask a particular question, when to look at a particular activity and think, 'Ahh, if I give them that piece of equipment now that is going to extend just that little bit further'.

In practice, Hannah was observed to scaffold children's learning on several occasions, for example at planning time:

Hannah: If you're not working with one of us and you're not sure what to do next, what could you do?
Edward: Look at the planning board.
Hannah: Brilliant, good boy. You could come and look at the planning board and think, 'Ooh yes! I haven't done that yet', and that helps you to remember all the things you could do.

Pamela said that she empowered children by asking for their ideas, listening and valuing their suggestions, and by actively deciding not to solve problems for them. Pamela avoided giving children solutions or answers, and preferred to 'wonder aloud' because she perceived that real learning is interactive and participatory, adding:

> I often try to, when I am questioning them I 'wonder why'. 'I wonder if you have got an answer to that?' so I wonder aloud as a role model and talk about their opinion so you know, 'So what's your opinion of this?' so that they know that their opinion is valued.

Commentary

Hannah and Pamela reflected Vygotsky's socio-cultural constructivist theory, which was shown by their understanding of children's learning taking place in a social context. Both teachers used language as a tool to help children construct and internalise knowledge, and both empowered children to make decisions, to build on their competencies, to follow their interests and try new experiences.

Both teachers assumed that the socio-cultural context of the classrooms was beneficial to children but neither had processes for children to question the practices or talk about any inequalities that may exist. Consequently any inequalities are likely to remain hidden from view and to be perpetuated. In classrooms where the principles of social justice are transgressed, the power of Vygotsky's theory to empower children may be annulled. Teachers who believe that the social context of learning is powerful may need to implement processes to ensure that it is a positive influence on children's behaviour.

It would be good to stop and consider your response to Pamela and Hannah.

Did any aspects of their theories match your own? Think about how different your views are and what difference it makes to the way you set up and maintain your classroom, and how you respond to children's behaviour.

The commentary stated that injustice may be part of a classroom context and may remain hidden from view. Do you agree? Have you ever experienced or seen injustice in classrooms? Try and be as specific as you can in describing the situation and how you felt about it.

Ellen

The fourth teacher, Ellen from the United Kingdom, reflected a theory of learning that was similar in many ways to Pamela and Hannah, however there were some important differences. Ellen's knowledge of children's learning was based on the importance of social justice and equality of opportunities to learn, which is sometimes called 'emancipatory constructivism' (Vandenboncoeur, 1997).

Frequently Ellen talked about issues surrounding the children's sense of power and the teacher's use of power. Her knowledge about the power and children's opportunities to learn had influenced her practice in many ways, which was shown when she said she aimed to make the classroom 'equal in terms of power, to be all at the same level'.

Like Hannah and Pamela, Ellen provided many opportunities for children to make decisions and act on their choices, however her reasons for doing so were a little different. Ellen wanted children to make choices because then power was shared equally between teachers and children. For example, children were able to decide whether or not to join an adult-led activity. Children made plans for the day when they arrived at school, and these were written or drawn in a special pad. Ellen respected their plans because she considered adult and child-initiated activities were equally important to children's learning.

Ellen believed that the learning environment had to be maintained in an orderly way so that it was predictable and responsive to the children's learning, which she explained:

> That is to do with empowerment I think. You know if they are going to feel empowered, they have got to know what's available and where it's going to be and they've got to know that they will always find it there. So you know that they won't find the scissors all over the classroom; they'll find them in the scissor-holes.

Similarly, Ellen made decisions about seating arrangements that were based on her notion of equity. At whole-group time she sat on the carpet with the children rather than on a chair and she reasoned:

> One of the things I am quite aware of is the height at which we sit, and I think that's so important, so when I want them to sit on the floor for a circle time I try and always sit on the floor as well ... generally if you want to engage in a kind of worthwhile conversation and talk to them about something, then I think that it is important to be at the same physical level.

Ellen believed that equity was established and conveyed to the children when teacher and children sat at the same level. Ellen said that she did not want to appear to be cross-questioning children at circle time, but wanted it to be a free-flowing discussion between all participants in the circle.

Ellen reflected her view of equity and the importance of the social context of learning when she reminded children about the needs of others:

> Sophie and Harriet, you're leaving Ben out of the circle, could you just move back so that you're not, because you've got your back to Ben haven't you Harriet? So that he doesn't feel left out.

Ellen's decisions about the way to manage small group learning experiences reflected her knowledge of equity. One learning experience was similar to the drawing and writing experience observed in Christine's class, however the theory guiding the teachers' practices resulted in differences in ways to manage the task.

Ellen followed-up a story she had read about 'Red Fox' by inviting children to draw a picture about it but no pressure was placed on children to participate in the experience. Ellen was available to scribe the story of their picture once they had completed their picture. Ellen sat at the same level as the children and she asked them where she could write the words and if she could put the title and date at the bottom of the page. Children were not hurried, and everything they said was accepted and written down. In conversation with one child, Sarah, Ellen asked:

> Do you want to tell me about your story?
> Tell me what to write.
> Anything else?

Sarah's picture had deviated from the Red Fox story, and her title was *Things that stuff wash in*, which Ellen accepted without comment. At one point Ellen wanted to clarify part of the picture with Sarah and the following interaction took place:

Sarah: That's animal things.
Ellen: What sort of animal things?
Sarah: Spider animal things.

Ellen wrote the words as Sarah dictated. After slow and careful work Sarah's story was completed as follows:

> Where the babies sleep
> in their bed.
> That's fireworks.
> That's the fox's bed.
> That is windy.
> The fox is asleep upstairs,
> the baby is frightened downstairs.
> The baby goes upstairs.
>
> The washing machine with

> the baby's clothes and the mummy's clothes.
> That is a squirrel.
> That's the animal things,
> a spider animal.
>
> Things that stuff wash in. Plates and things.

Ellen maintained that it would have been 'totally inappropriate' to try and remain focused on the story of Red Fox when Sarah's story had moved away from it. Ellen said that the story was meaningful to Sarah and that it was important for her to have ownership of her work because, 'they are not doing it for the teacher, they are doing it for themselves'.

Commentary

Ellen's theory of teaching and learning included her ideas of social justice. Ellen sought to redistribute power within the classroom and to achieve an equitable balance between adults and children. She wanted all children to have equal opportunities to participate in quality learning experiences, and she critically reflected on her practice, which included her biases. Ellen showed that she engaged in a process of reflecting on her practice in order to provide a fair and responsive classroom environment that gave all children an equal opportunity to learn.

How do you respond to Ellen's theory that everything, even physical position such as sitting at the same level as the children, sends important messages to children about empowerment?

Do you think that things like seating position matter? Why or why not?

More importantly, do you think that children and teachers should be 'equal'?

Think about the different strategies that Ellen and Christine used when they asked children to dictate a story that was scribed by the teacher. Their strategies related to their theories of teaching and learning.

What is your response to the two sets of strategies? How might these strategies influence children's feelings of self-efficacy?

Now begin to write down your own theory of teaching and learning, and try to make some direct links between your theory and how you manage children's behaviour.

Summary

My aim is to help you begin to look at the theories you hold because making your theories explicit may help you make sense of your actions as a teacher. It is worth thinking about the four teachers and having a guess at the types of relationships they develop with the children they teach.

Think about the first, teacher, Christine and her view that children's development occurs within the individual. One problem with this view is that teachers do not examine the *context* of children's behaviour. However, this book takes the view that children's behaviour cannot be separated from the context. Therefore, understanding children's behaviour means analysing the context, which is often a difficult process but one that can lead to positive change.

A great deal of teachers' knowledge is implicit knowledge. The advantage of talking about knowledge is that it allows teachers to update and change it, in view of new facts, concepts and information. Teachers may realise that they hold contradictory values when they talk with other professionals. Talking and reflecting can help teachers reshape their knowledge to allow them to achieve their aims. In some schools teaching colleagues visit each other's classrooms to observe and give feedback to their peers. Reflective conversations that follow peer observations can help teachers to realise that new ways of teaching and learning do not always fit with what they know about how children should behave in classrooms. Reflective conversations sometimes enable teaching colleagues to clarify and change some of their taken for granted assumptions.

Teachers who reflect on their knowledge in order to understand children's troublesome behaviour find that there are shifts in their perceptions, feelings, and expectations. They find that they gain new insights into the classroom context that is supporting inappropriate behaviour. Teachers who work through the process of exploring what they know about teaching and learning with a colleague find that the process becomes an enjoyable part of their professional development.

Prejudice and bias is still part of some education systems, as William's story showed in this chapter. Many teachers have found it helpful to reflect on what they know and take that first step to working differently in the classroom (Siraj-Blatchford, 1994). Teachers who understand how justice is eroded will be able to counter it and will be able to provide classrooms that set the scene for children's appropriate classroom behaviour.

Chapter 4

Children and troublesome behaviour

> People just keeped on talking to me and making me talk.
>
> (Tom, 7 years)

In the previous chapter I focused on the teacher, in this chapter I shift the emphasis to the child. I present case studies of three boys whose troublesome behaviours had caused many problems, over a long period of time, to them, their teachers and their classmates. The purpose of this chapter is to show how children adapt to their contextual challenges, and show how relationships between children and teachers act as zones of proximal development for children's educational and social outcomes. As you read the children's stories, try to put yourself in their shoes. Try asking yourself:

- what would it be like going to school each day for this child?
- what is life like for their teachers and the thirty or so children in each class?
- how could classroom life be different? What would make the difference?

I hope the case studies will provoke you to question whether the schools were demonstrating evidence-based practice, and if not, what seemed to guide their decisions.

The chapter provides some information about the case study approach, which is a research strategy that teachers can use to help them investigate phenomena in their classrooms. I hope that these case studies will encourage you to start talking seriously to the children you teach, because if we really want to know something about somebody (regardless of their age) then we should ask them. Children know a great deal about classroom behaviour and we need to keep talking to them about their understandings, because what children know can influence what teachers know about the classroom.

The aim of the case studies was to understand more about the way children thought about aspects of their behaviours and experiences in the classroom and playground. Gerovich (1999) wanted to explore children's understandings and to see how their views about their behaviour fitted with observations of their experiences. The participants were three seven-year-old boys who had been diagnosed with attention deficit hyperactivity disorder (ADHD) and prescribed medication to enable them to behave appropriately and manage school life.

The study took place in a metropolitan area of one Australian city at a time when there was a rapid increase in the number of children being diagnosed as ADHD and taking prescribed medication to enable them to control their behaviour. Critics suggested that the condition was being over-diagnosed and that children were exhibiting very troublesome classroom behaviours for a range of different reasons. Although diagnosis was variable, children with ADHD-type behaviour experience many difficulties in classrooms; these included poor peer relationships and low levels of social skills. The case studies provide a picture of the children's learning relationships and the opportunities they offer for the children's behaviours.

Conducting a case study

Teachers can use the case study method to investigate phenomena in their own classrooms. However, most teachers need collegial support to conduct this type of research as it relies on observations, field notes, and interviews, which are time-consuming. Schools tend to be able to make arrangements for teachers to research together when they believe that the outcomes will benefit the school. The following section explains some key points of constructing case studies, and uses the research study to be reported here as an example.

In general, studying one or more cases is a valuable way to advance understanding of difficulties, such as troublesome behaviour. Each case has certain features, patterns and boundaries that can be revealed through repeated observations (Stake, 1994). Understanding the features of the case can contribute to teachers' theories; for example, it can inform how they explain children's behaviour in order to make change. Findings from a case study can ensure that evidence-based practice is planned and implemented in schools.

The methods used for these case studies included observing in the classroom and interviewing children, teachers, principals and parents. The fieldwork requires the researcher to gather qualitative and quantitative evidence and to keep observing until no new information is forthcoming. The combination of quantitative and qualitative data allowed the features, patterns, and boundaries of the cases to be identified.

In the study to be reported, field notes documented sequences of behaviour so that interpretations could be made about the children's relationships within each context. The field notes consisted of observations in the form of running records that were conducted in the classroom each day for at least sixty minutes over a four-week period. When making running records the observer focused on one child, and wrote down everything that the child did and said in a given period; this could be five minutes or 30 minutes, depending on the context. For example, the observer might be recording a five-minute transition from seats to recess, or a whole group time that lasted for 20 minutes.

The running records enabled the observer to identify typical behaviours used by the child, and it revealed the sequence of interactions and consequences. The researcher attended the classroom and school to observe the child at different times of the day in different types of activities. For example, observations were conducted during whole group mat time, individual seatwork, transitions, music, physical education, lunchtime and recess.

Running records were made until no new behaviours were recorded. The information gathered in the running record was used to identify typical behaviours used by the child. Care was taken to record observed behaviour only and to use objective language. These behaviours were then recorded on an observation sheet, which allowed the researcher to observe and document the frequency of a particular behaviour in a systematic way. An example of an observation sheet that is based on behaviours identified from a running record is shown in Figure 4.1

Observations focused on and documented the frequency of a particular behaviour, for example, how many times a child made noises in a 20-minute period. Frequencies allow comparisons between elements to be made, for example, the child's noise-making behaviour during seatwork compared with group work.

Several interviews were conducted with the children, following an observation. The interview questions were based on the field notes and probed

Name of child Tom ______________ Date and Time of observation ______________
Name of Observer ______________ Context ______________

Behaviour — Frequency in five-minute intervals

Behaviour	5 mins	5 mins	5 mins	5 mins	5 mins
Calling out					
Whistling					
Sounds: such as ahhh (s); tongue clicks (tc)					
Singing					
Talking to other children					
Touching others and their possessions					
Body noises: clicking fingers (cf); foot tapping (ft); passing wind (pw)					

Figure 4.1 *Observation sheet to record the frequency of particular behaviours.*

the child's perception of his behaviour and his rationale for it. For example, the researcher noted that one child tended to make noises when exhibiting troublesome behaviour, and so asked him a question about noise-making behaviour. No attempt was made to be consistent across the cases, for example, the other two children were not asked about making noises because that wasn't part of their repertoire of troublesome behaviours.

In two of the cases, interviews were conducted until saturation point had been reached, which means that no new information was forthcoming from the children. However, one of the children refused to cooperate in the interview sessions, and in the end the researcher was only able to conduct one interview in any depth.

Case study one – Tom

Tom lived at home with his mother and 13-year-old brother. Tom's mother reported that he had been diagnosed with ADHD as a six year old and placed on medication to control his aggressive behaviour. The diagnosis of ADHD was preceded by a history of behaviour problems. Tom's mother described him as 'extremely overactive' since the age of two years. Tom attended pre-primary when he was five years old and his teacher described his peer relationships as 'extremely negative'.

When Tom was six, two serious incidents led to his referral to a paediatrician and the subsequent diagnosis of ADHD. First, he smashed a glass window with his fist, second, threw a brick at his brother that had hit him on the head. Tom's mother said she had regular contact with the school and usually spoke to Tom's class teacher about three times a week. Tom's mother said that she had an interview at the beginning of each school term with the principal and class teacher.

Tom attended the local primary school and there were 23 children in his class. Tom was one of three children in the class who were diagnosed as ADHD and who took medication for the condition. The school principal described Tom as 'very bright', but emphasised that his behaviour was a 'constant source of concern'. The principal assisted the teacher when particular problems came up but otherwise did not have regular contact with Tom.

The principal commented that she could not understand why Tom should still misbehave because he had been diagnosed and medicated 'correctly'. The school had little background information about Tom or his family, and no information about Tom's father. Tom's teacher had little to say about him, but she commented that, 'Tom can be a very irritating child, and he always has to have the last word'.

Observations in the classroom showed that Tom attracted a great deal of negative attention from the teacher and his peers. For example, frequently he was the last child to follow the teacher's instructions and many times he responded only briefly, which led to the teacher giving him individual and specific instructions of increasing strength. A typical example of the interactions that characterised his day occurred when the teacher called all the children to the mat:

> Tom was the last child to join the group as he walked slowly across the room on his own. He sat on his feet at the back of the group with his fingers in his mouth and looked around the room as several children continued to talk. He looked at the teacher as she asked the children to sit quietly and listen, then she began speaking to individual children about their word quota numbers. Tom knelt up on his knees and looked around the room with his fingers in his mouth. The teacher continued to speak to individuals while several children began talking to each other. Tom sat down on his feet and turned to talk quietly to Blake, who was sitting next to him. Blake did not answer but Tom continued to speak to him. The teacher looked at Tom and said, 'Tom, come and sit over here please', then pointed to a space near her chair, Tom stood up and walked around the back of the group. He sat with his legs crossed near the teacher and looked at her as she leaned forward and spoke quietly to him. The teacher continued to speak to other individuals, and Tom knelt up on his knees and looked around the room. The teacher frowned as she looked at Tom and said, 'Tom! Sit on your bottom and cross your legs now!' Tom responded immediately.

When Tom was asked about the rules at group time he said:

Tom: Um, you have to sit on the floor with your legs crossed.
Interviewer: Do you always sit with your legs crossed?
Tom: Yes, but only when I'm at the back I don't
Interviewer: How do you sit at the back?
Tom: Um, sometimes I kneel, no, but because sometimes I really can't *see*.

Tom showed his knowledge of the group time rules and gave reasons when he didn't keep them. Similarly, he showed his knowledge of the 'hands up to speak' rule, which he was observed to keep 50 per cent of the time:

Tom: You can put your hand up, but sometimes not really many people get choosed to answer.
Interviewer: Do you ever call out answers?
Tom: Well, not really, 'cause that's not what you really do.

Tom made noises by whistling, singing or calling out which resulted in a great deal of teacher and peer attention. Tom made noises frequently during individual seatwork sessions when the children had been set work that they needed to complete. For example, during seatwork the teacher asked the class a question:

> Tom sat in his chair and made comments and noises like 'Aha. Aha' then looked at the teacher and took his jumper off and wrapped it around his head. The teacher continued to speak to the group as Tom made high-pitched singing noises. Several children commented about Tom's noises and the teacher said, 'Tom is being very annoying today and I'm trying to ignore his silly and bad behaviour'.

Often, the negative interactions were prolonged and followed a typical pattern, which is shown in Figure 4.2.

This pattern is seen in the following example when the children had told the teacher that Tom was making noises:

> The teacher said, 'Tom! Stop this nonsense at once!' and she praised several children for sitting nicely. Tom looked at those children as he cupped his hands over his mouth and began singing quietly. The teacher said, 'TOM! Decide whether you're going to sit out or join in the group without singing. I will not have you being so inconsiderate to the other children!'

When Tom was asked about making noises in class he seemed reluctant to answer:

Tom: What, do you mean like um, if um, like you um, want to tell the um, teacher a answer?

Interviewer: No. I mean do you ever make noises that bother the teacher or the other children in your class?

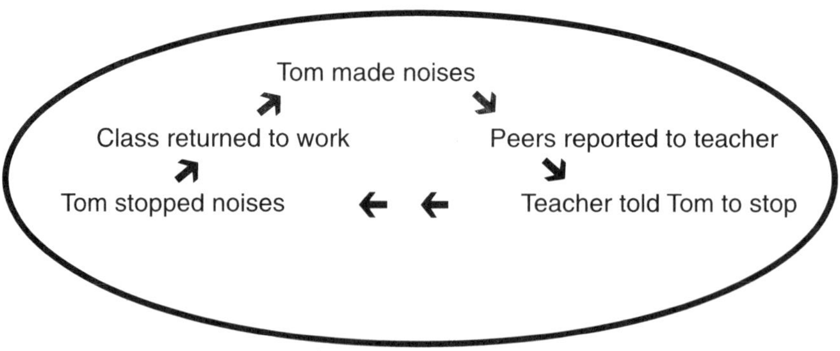

Figure 4.2 Pattern of behaviour in the classroom.

Tom: Oh, like whistling or that?
Interviewer: Yes, that's right.
Tom: Well, you're not really meant to do things like that really.
Interviewer: Yes, I know. But do you ever do that?
Tom: I think it's nearly lunchtime.

Quite often during the observation period Tom did not complete his seatwork tasks independently and his behaviour attracted the teacher's rebukes. On one occasion the teacher stood behind Tom's chair for ten minutes but her presence seemed to provide Tom with little help. After ten minutes of struggle, the teacher wrote 'unable to complete' across the top of his worksheet, then dated and filed it without comment.

Most of Tom's interactions with his classroom teacher appeared to be negative, and these adverse interactions reflected his seemingly constant interruptions to the classroom process, seen in the following example when the class were engaged in individual seatwork. Tom had been sent outside for calling out and 'interfering' with other children and five minutes later the teacher invited Tom to rejoin the class:

> Tom walked to his desk and knelt in his chair. He turned to face his neighbour, Libby, and put his jumper on her head. Libby pushed the jumper away without talking and the teacher called to Tom, 'TOM! Stop that now and get on with your work'. Tom began speaking to Libby who did not look at him or respond. Then Tom moved his maths book around his desk and onto Libby's desk, she said quietly, 'Stop it Tom'. The teacher called to Tom, 'Leave the room Tom. I will not have you disrupting this classroom any more. Just stop acting like an idiot!' Tom looked at his teacher as he walked towards the door, then he sat outside the room with his legs crossed and fingers in his mouth.

Later the interviewer asked Tom to talk about the things that had happened in the day that he wasn't pleased about and he did not talk about his own behaviour:

Tom: Um the um. I tried my best still but I did, but people just keeped on um talking to me and making me talk. … Um someone made me talk … Libby, but um um I just talked a tiny, a about, one um about um, about talked about one thing very quick and it was about one second …

How often did Tom misbehave?

Early in the observations, the researcher had the feeling that Tom was uncompliant almost all the time as he attracted a great deal of negative attention from the teacher and his classmates. However, analysis of timed observations showed that the observer's 'gut feel' was incorrect: Tom actually complied with 65 per cent of the teacher's instructions, leaving 35 per cent of instructions that he ignored or was slow to follow.

We were interested to see what types of behaviour attracted the teacher's attention. Analysis of Tom's acts of uncompliant behaviour showed that the behaviours that attracted 68 per cent of the teacher's rebukes were:

Group Time:	Frequent changes in sitting position;
Group/Seat Time:	Calling out inappropriately, mostly by making noises such as whistling or other sounds;
Seatwork:	Hindering others from learning, such as touching them, for example, putting his jumper on a peer's head or touching their work.

Detailed analysis of the Tom's responses to the teacher's individual and group instructions showed that his numerous acts of *compliance* tended to be unnoticed, apparently ignored, or at least unmentioned by his teacher.

The interviewer sought to probe Tom's knowledge of his teacher's expectations in an effort to find out if Tom knew what behaviour pleased the teacher. Tom was able to name the classroom rules and his teacher's expectations and he added:

Tom:	You need to really always try your hardest and do your best work
Interviewer:	mmm, anything else?
Tom:	Um, no.
Interviewer:	What about if another child talks to you or annoys you during class?
Tom:	You can just say one thing that's really important and for just about one minute or two seconds, and that's what I do.
Interviewer:	What about if someone bothers you?
Tom:	Well, I just don't, don't, I just do my work and ignore them.

Behaviour with other teachers

It was observed that Tom and the music specialist interacted positively. The music specialist was observed to praise, encourage and support Tom's compliant behaviour and his level of compliance rose to more than 85 per cent during music. A typical example of a positive interaction was seen when the teacher had to speak to three children who were arguing about not having enough room:

> Tom called, 'Ms James, Ms James!' The music specialist turned to face Tom and said, 'Yes Tom?' and Tom replied 'I. I just um moved from over

> there because I um I um didn't have very much room'. The music specialist smiled and commented, 'That's very sensible Tom. I wish these three people could be as sensible as you, instead of pushing each other, just move to another spot'. Tom smiled at the teacher and joined in with the next activity.

This interaction showed that Tom was able to get the teacher's attention to report a positive act, and that the teacher affirmed his good behaviour. Tom was awarded a special certificate following a successful music lesson. Later the interviewer asked him what had helped him get the award:

Tom: Ahhh, what made me do it?
Interviewer: Oh okay. What made you do it?
Tom: Um I think the tablets, have, have made me um settle down today, and and be um, very um, kind to people.

As this exchange shows, Tom credited his medication with his good behaviour, but he tended to blame others for his troublesome behaviour:

Interviewer: So what kinds of things happened yesterday that you weren't pleased about?
Tom: Yesterday Libby, she um just keeped on making me talk and talk and talk and talk. And making me not finish my work. But today I tried, um to ignore her.

Outside the classroom

Observations included Tom's interactions with his peers in the classroom and playground, and showed that the majority of Tom's attempts to interact were ignored. A poignant and typical example occurred when the children were practising skipping outside with the classroom teacher.

> Tom stopped near a group of children who were talking about how many skips they could do, and Tom said, 'Oh yeah. I can do that' and he skipped away to show them. Then he turned around and called to the children and his teacher, 'Did you see that? I did eight! Did you see?' but neither teacher nor peers looked in his direction or responded to him.

Tom's lack of positive interaction during class time was reflected in the playground, where he appeared to have few friends. Interview material showed that Tom was well aware of his difficulties and he showed good knowledge about friendship:

Interviewer: ... What kind of things do friends do together?
Tom: Um play wiv ya. and be nice to ya. And and and, and they um,

	when when people like um me sometimes have um not no friends to play wiv. they can um, help help people, and they can um play wiv you.
Interviewer:	Yes, that's very true. And what other things do friends do?
Tom:	Um. Maybe they might, help people when um they're feeling a bit sad and they've got no friends, like um me.

The interviewer showed Tom some pictures of a boy who wanted to join a game, and Tom was asked what the boy could say or do to get to play:

Tom:	He could say, um, ... well I've got no friends
Interviewer:	And if they said to him 'Well, why haven't you got any?
Tom:	Um 'cause no-one wants to play wiv me.
Interviewer:	And why not?
Tom:	Mmm 'cause they don't want um um play wiv me. Cause they may be think um um I'm always naughty ...
Interviewer:	Ohh!
Tom	... when he's not!

Commentary

Tom's behaviour could be explained in many different ways and from several different perspectives. Explanations could be used to find some positive ways to help this boy develop more fulfilling relationships at school. Some researchers may explain Tom's behaviour by saying that ADHD children are emotionally immature or that primary age children have no qualms about rejecting peers who are self-absorbed, uncooperative, disruptive or hostile (Cole and Chan, 1994). However, the systems model offers different insights.

Observations of Tom's life at school showed it was filled with some positive and many negative events that shaped and were shaped by his history, cognitions and experiences. Tom talked about the formal and informal rules that governed classroom behaviour and friendships, but this knowledge did not seem to help him demonstrate acceptable classroom behaviour or develop friendships. Tom's behaviour can be understood by seeing it as his adaptation to elements in the system. How can we interpret Tom's goal of adaptation? It seems reasonable to infer that avoiding being ignored was high on the list, possibly because being ignored left Tom with the fear of being abandoned, an ever-present danger for some vulnerable children.

After analysing the observation data, it was evident that Tom tended to be ignored by the group when he was compliant but he drew a great deal of attention when he was infringing the rules. Therefore, it seems that relationships between Tom, his classroom teacher and peers were based partly on a struggle about gaining and withholding attention.

In seeking to change Tom's behaviour at school, we need to ask about the contexts for his development, and the opportunities being provided to help him achieve his educational and social potentials. One inference is that the diagnosis of ADHD to account for Tom's behaviour had been an influential context for his development. The ADHD diagnosis led to a medical approach to treatment and placed Tom squarely in the arena of individual deficit. The diagnosis meant that Tom's troublesome behaviour was located within Tom, and it deflected attention away from his relationships with his mother and older brother, the circumstances of his family or type of resources they were able to provide for Tom.

It seems that the medical diagnosis of ADHD halted any investigation of the circumstances that led Tom to throw a brick at his brother or punch his fist through a glass window. Neither Tom's mother nor the school offered any information about Tom's father or the circumstances or timing of his separation from the family or subsequent contact. It seemed that little was known by the school about the level of a support system for the family, such as Church or social clubs, the neighbourhood, or more formal government agencies.

It is possible that the diagnosis of ADHD contributed to the erosion of social justice for Tom because it cloaked other ways of seeing his behaviour, for example, no attempt was made to understand the relationships between Tom, his peers and his teacher. The inequities of the classroom were obscured from the principal and teacher not because they were being unprofessional, but because they believed that *this ADHD child* behaved in puzzling ways. The medical diagnosis of Tom's behaviour was accepted without question by the staff who relied on his medication to help him conform to the teacher's expectations.

Acceptance of the ADHD diagnosis precluded his teacher from investigating the classroom dynamics that were providing an important context for Tom's behaviour. One interpretation of the case study material is that the context offered little to help Tom to adapt his behaviour and achieve his potentials. It seemed that Tom, his peers and the teacher had created a context that was hostile to Tom, and he gained recognition from others when he was characterised as the 'naughty boy' of the classroom. Tom's relationships at school depended on him being uncompliant, which enabled his peers to reject him. Therefore it is concluded that the context supported Tom's maladaptive behaviour.

In fact there were many times during the school day when Tom responded quickly and positively to the teacher's instructions, however there were repeated examples of protracted troublesome behaviours. Why did Tom's compliant behaviour rise to 85 per cent with the music specialist? Again there may be several ways to explain the difference:

- Tom has a history of enjoying music, so he brought some positive expectations to the music class.

- The music teacher stimulated a positive context for his development with her choice of learning experiences, ways of involving the children, methods, or the way she organised active and passive learning experiences.
- Tom's compliant behaviour may have been his adaptation to a supportive relationship with the music teacher.

It seems fair to assume that Tom, the teacher, his peers, and the school principal developed a powerful set of shared cognitions about Tom. It is reasonable to infer that the cognitions might include the following:

Tom's **peers** know Tom – he's the boy with whom nobody wants to play because he's naughty. He's the pest, the one they don't like, and the one that the teacher doesn't like. He's the boy who's *always* been naughty, ever since pre-primary. He's never invited to birthday parties.

The **teacher** knows Tom – he is the boy who makes her day a misery. Tom is the boy who *never* attends or follows her instructions and who drives her crazy with his constant attention-seeking behaviour. He's the boy who tires her out, and she's counting the weeks till the end of the school year when it's 'Goodbye Tom'!

The **school principal** knows Tom – he's the ADHD boy who is causing her teacher lots of hassles that she gripes about in the staff room. He's the boy she has to deal with from time to time because of playground problems. He's the boy whose mother she sees at the beginning of each term, and he's the boy who's not responding to his medication, which might mean there is something else wrong with him.

Tom knows about himself too – he's the boy who feels 'a bit sad' because he's got 'no friends'. He's the boy with whom nobody wants to play because they think 'I'm always naughty'. He's the boy who takes tablets that make him good and has classmates who make him bad.

Tom uses his cognitions to respond to contextual challenges that have the potential to be damaging for him. Tom has developed some pessimistic thinking about himself and his relationships with his peers and teachers (Seligman, 1995). Pessimistic thinking leads to powerlessness because children think that problems are permanent and beyond their control to change.

Pessimistic thinking is a habit or disposition of mind that disempowers children in the face of difficulties because they think there is nothing *they* can do about their problems. For example, when Tom says that other children make him naughty then he will find it difficult to think about what is in *his* power to change. Tom's cognitions showed little optimistic thinking, which helps children to see their difficulties as being temporary, specific to a particular problem and within their power to change.

The cognitions of the teacher and children shape and are shaped by *the relationships* that are made possible in the school and classroom context. Opportunities for relationships have been established over time and with regard to Tom's history. When Tom finishes the year and progresses to his third year of schooling, Tom and the group will take a history that has established Tom as the 'naughty boy'.

It appears that the relationships available in the context have been built on Tom behaving in an uncompliant way. Observations showed that Tom tended to be ignored when he was compliant; when he appeared to become invisible in the group. We need to consider what this means for his daily behaviours. Remember that in Tom's view to answer a question, 'you can put your hand up, but sometimes not really many people get choosed to answer'. The context tended to ignore Tom when he had his hand up, but paid him a great deal of attention when he was uncompliant. We need to ask why Tom's behaviour was important to the group and what group function it played. The school did not investigate this matter partly because Tom's behaviour was constructed on the grounds that his behaviour was a medical condition, which occurred within the individual and therefore was treated *within* the individual by medication.

Case study two – Jack

Seven-year-old Jack lived with his parents and was the second child with three sisters aged 10 years, two years and six months. He attended a class of 27 children that included another boy who was being assessed for a behavioural disorder.

Jack's mother reported that he was a 'very active' toddler who became an aggressive four-year-old. His mother said that Jack was particularly aggressive towards her, saying that he hit and punched her. Jack's mother said that he often went to her wardrobe and cut her clothes with scissors. His mother said he was disruptive in pre-primary, and his parents had sought help after he was involved in an incident that involved the police when he was six years old.

Jack was assessed by a paediatrician, was diagnosed with ADHD and began medication. Jack's mother said she was reluctant to give him medication and that he took it only during school hours. His mother said that occasionally she sent him to school without medication in order to monitor his behaviour. Jack's mother organised for him to receive 'kinesiology therapy' and she reported that it was 'helping him relax and behave less aggressively'. He had not been involved in any behaviour management programme, and no family intervention had taken place.

The school principal noted that Jack had changed greatly since he began taking medication, and that he was far less aggressive and disruptive in class. The principal praised the classroom teacher and said that she had persevered through 'very trying times'.

The classroom teacher commented that Jack was 'very average' academically but was 'extremely likeable'. She noted that Jack was a popular child with an 'appealing personality'. The teacher said that she was aware that Jack manipulated her and monopolised her time in class, which she said was 'a trap' that she 'constantly fell into' and she had to make herself aware of it continually.

The teacher said that Jack's concentration was 'limited' and that without medication he was disinterested in school work and he was 'extremely disruptive' in class. The teacher said that the principal supported her 100 per cent and worked closely with her on all matters concerning Jack.

It was intended to use the same procedure for Jack's case study as the other children in the study, however, Jack refused to be interviewed during the study, and although he finally agreed to one interview, he was not cooperative and contributed very little. Jack's reluctance meant that we could not document his cognitions about several important aspects of the classroom, although he did talk about his views of friendship and social status.

Teacher–child interactions

Classroom observations showed that Jack's behaviour captured the teacher's attention and she responded quickly to him. Findings showed that 47 per cent of the interactions between Jack and his teacher were positive, and 53 per cent were negative. However, these figures do not adequately reflect the attention demanded by Jack, as the teacher ignored many of Jack's uncompliant acts, particularly for minor infringements such as calling out at group time. It was observed that his teacher responded quickly and positively when he complied with the rules. However, 43 per cent of observed interactions between Jack and his teachers resulted from:

- moving and fidgeting;
- calling out during seatwork;
- being off task or behaving inappropriately during activities;
- stopping others from working.

Observations in the classroom suggested that Jack's level of compliance with the class rules was influenced by the reward or punishment promised by the teacher. For example, Jack complied with the teacher's instructions when she chose children to go to lunch:

> Jack quickly crawled forward and sat directly in front of the teacher with his legs crossed and arms folded. The teacher leaned forward and whispered to him 'Go and get your lunch from your bag'. Jack immediately crawled over to his bag at the back of the room.

At times, Jack ignored the teacher's instructions, particularly when a reward or incentive was not offered. On some occasions when Jack ignored a direct instruction, the teacher issued one or two warnings, and then operated a 'time out' system. Jack earned minutes of time out for not following the teacher's instructions, but the system also operated in reverse, so that minutes could be removed if Jack complied with the rules later. Time out was used as a punishment, as Jack was made to miss the relevant minutes of playtime or lunchtime by sitting out in his classroom or at the principal's office.

At times, in the observer's opinion, Jack appeared to be deliberately defiant rather than impulsive, as is seen in the following example, which occurred during a mat session when Jack crawled out of the circle to the front of the room to get a tissue:

> The teacher continued to explain the maths activity to the children as Jack slowly walked back towards the mat area. The teacher looked at Jack and said, 'Jack, come and sit down'. Jack sat outside the circle near a table containing games and building materials. The teacher continued to speak to the group as Jack began playing with a container of cubes under the table. The teacher warned Jack that he was earning time out for himself. Jack continued to play with the cubes as the teacher looked at him and said, 'Two'. Jack asked 'What?' and the teacher replied, 'Two minutes'. Another child, Danny, was sent to sit at his desk for calling out and Jack looked at him and then continued to play with the cubes. The teacher said, 'Three'. I will continue to add on until you stop playing and join in with our group'. Jack did not look at the teacher as he continued to build with the blocks. The teacher asked the children to return to their desks and Jack put the blocks away and walked to his seat. His name and five time out minutes were recorded on the board.

As this observation showed, Jack ignored a direct instruction to sit down and he then received a warning about earning 'time out'. Jack ignored the warning but when his teacher called out 'two', he appeared not to understand what she meant although the teacher had used the procedure many times in the past. Jack's teacher responded to his question by explaining about time out.

Later in the session the teacher rewarded Jack's compliant behaviour:

> Jack sat facing his desk with his feet on the floor. He opened his maths pad and folded his arms on the desk. Kate, Jack's neighbour, was not at her desk and Jack leaned across and opened her maths pad too, then he quickly folded his arms again and looked at the teacher as she spoke to the group. The teacher praised Jack for sitting and waiting so quietly and removed a time out minute from the board as she commented, 'Now you're back to four'. Jack continued to sit with his arms folded as he looked at the teacher.

Jack continued to exhibit compliant behaviour that led to more of the time out minutes to be neutralised. Observations showed that he appeared to be aware of the classroom rules, such as not calling out and putting hands up for a turn to speak. Findings showed that he complied with 58 per cent of his teachers' direct instructions.

Jack attracted the attention of his peers and teachers frequently and in a variety of ways. For example, Jack was engaged in artwork:

> Jack rolled red paint back and forth on the glass surface, then placed a sheet of paper on the wet paint. He rubbed his hands across the paper and called out, 'Oh my God! Come and look at this you guys'. Three children working nearby turned around and looked at Jack's print. The teacher called Jack to her and showed him the next step in the process.

During the observations, the observer assessed Jack's responses as being deliberately slow and there were many times when he was the focus of both teacher and peer attention while he exhibited uncompliant behaviour. An example was seen when the children were sitting in a circle and the teacher asked the group a question:

> Jack looked at Kate who had been selected to answer, and then he turned and crawled to the side door that the wind had blown open. He pushed the door closed and asked in a shaky voice, 'Who's there ...?' The children laughed, and Jack laughed too and continued to make comments as the door blew open again and he pushed it closed again. The teacher asked Jack to rejoin the group. Jack pushed the door one last time, made another comment, walked back to the circle and sat in his place.

Jack's confronting behaviour slowed down teaching time but it did not evoke negative responses from his peers or teacher. Observation data showed that Jack's classmates responded with laughter to his defiant behaviour several times and the teacher ignored this behaviour. During a lesson Jack had not followed the teacher's instructions and a little while later he ignored a further instruction:

> Jack sat with his legs cross and called out comments as the teacher called children's names to go to lunch. She looked at him as she continued to call children's names. Jack began speaking to child near him and he replied quietly. The teacher asked Jack and four other children who had not followed her instructions earlier to come to her. Jack stood up and walked towards the teacher but then continued to walk past her towards the classrooms where the children had gone to lunch. The children laughed but the teacher did not look at Jack or speak to him.

At times Jack's compliant behaviour received praise or reward from his teachers but he did not display his emotions. For example, Jack had completed a 'tidying-up task' for the teacher and had earned two points,

> Timothy turned and looked at Jack saying, 'Oh wow!' Jack did not look at Timothy or the teacher but continued with his task. The teacher dismissed the children for recess and praised Jack for having cleaned the desks so well. Jack picked up his jumper and walked with two classmates back to his room as they all talked to each other about Jack's artwork.

In trouble

By contrast, Jack was observed to react verbally when he had attracted a reprimand or had to face the consequences of his uncompliant behaviour. At times Jack's uncompliant behaviour in the classroom escalated to open defiance. An example occurred on one occasion when he had been told to go to the office during the lunch break because of his earlier challenging behaviour:

> Jack did not look at the teacher as he shouted, 'I'm not going to the office. I'm NOT!' The teacher dismissed the children and Jack stood up and walked to the playground. Later the teacher signalled for Jack to leave his football game and come to her. He shook his head and walked away to continue the game. At the end of lunchtime Jack walked to his classroom and sat at the side of his peers. He looked at the teacher as she approached the group but did not notice the principal approaching from behind him. The principal took Jack's arm and pulled him to his feet without speaking and guided him to a nearby bench. The principal spoke to Jack who began to cry. The principal spoke to Jack for ten minutes and then he returned to the classroom.

Friendship

There was ample evidence to suggest that Jack was a popular classmate, in spite of his inappropriate behaviour. During one session when children were asked to find a partner it was observed that four different children approached him. Observations showed that Jack initiated 72 per cent of peer interactions and 86 per cent received positive responses. Jack was happy to talk about his friends to the interviewer and appeared to be confident about his social status. However, Jack appeared to find it hard to talk about friendship apart from the fact it meant that children played together:

Interviewer: Can you think of things that you do with your friends?
Jack: Like, I play football and like that.
Interviewer: Yes. What other things do you do with your friends?
Jack: I play ... guns and Power Rangers. But that's something we play in the playground. That's about it, I do.
Interviewer: Do you share things with your friends?

Jack: Yeah.
Interviewer: What kind of things do friends share?
Jack: Everything.

Jack expressed some knowledge about how to join a game:

Jack: Say 'excuse me'.
Interviewer: So just say 'excuse me'.
Jack: Mmm 'Can I join in playing football?'
Interviewer: And if they said no to him, what else could he either say or do to join in that game?
Jack: Um... go to the teacher.
Interviewer: Oh right, and what would he say?
Jack: He could say that those two boys won't let me play football with them.
Interviewer: Do you think that would help?
Jack: Yeah.
Interviewer: Has that ever happened to you – where you'd like to join in and someone said 'no'.
Jack: Yeah, but um I don't, I fight them back.
Interviewer: Oh, and then do they let you join in?
Jack: Yeah, 'cause like I just say how old I am, and they'll say okay then.

Observations showed that Jacked engaged with three other children during the lunch breaks, and he played football with them without incident. Jack's apparent good relationships in the playground were reflected in his classroom interactions, which were typified by the following interaction:

> Jack tossed Patrick his eraser but it landed on the floor. Jack got out of his chair, walked behind Patrick, picked up the eraser and placed it on the desk in front of Patrick, who said, 'Oh thanks Jack'. Jack smiled and returned to his desk and then continued to write.

Commentary

As described in this overview of the case study, Jack evidenced uncompliant behaviour in the classroom and playground, and some could be described as acts of defiance. The task now is to use the systems model to inform our interpretations of Jack's behaviour, and to ascertain whether the school system was high or low in opportunities that promoted adaptive behaviour. The idea is not to find fault or lay blame, but to understand that Jack's behaviour resulted from interactions between elements and units in the family–school system, as well as the 'within child' system.

It seems reasonable to conclude that Jack's personality was an element that influenced his relationships in the system, as his teacher described him as 'likeable' and observations showed that children were attracted to him and sought his company. It seemed that he knew how to please his peers even though he appeared to have difficulty expressing his cognitions about friends and friendships.

Jack's aggression towards his mother, and her apparent acceptance of it, could reflect a coercive attachment relationship involving the aversive use of power, but little is known about his relationship with her, his father or his siblings. Jack's mother did not support the use of medication fully, and did not use it out of school hours. She sought alternative non-scientific therapies to help Jack, although she gives Jack his medication on most school days. Little is known about the decision to send Jack to kinesiology therapy or what Jack understood by this intervention. However it indicates that Jack's mother believed that ADHD could be treated with intervention other than medication, and that relaxation was beneficial.

Little was said about Jack's parents' relationship with the school and it seemed that his father had little contact with the teacher or principal. It would be important to know whether Jack's father was invited to attend school meetings and if meetings were arranged out of work times. Relationships between the school and Jack's father could provide a useful context for his development.

What relationships provided opportunities for Jack's adaptive behaviour at school? One interpretation of the case study material suggests that aspects of the classroom context supported Jack's troublesome and defiant behaviours. At times, Jack defied the teacher's authority, for example, when he ignored her instruction to go to the office, or to leave the football game and come to her. However, by and large Jack's defiance met no logical consequence and it often resulted in him getting what he wanted. For example, he wanted to play football, and he did play football. His defiant behaviour meant he had to listen to the principal 'telling off' for ten minutes, which meant he missed out on the individual seatworkwork that he did not like.

The teacher encouraged and praised Jack regularly in order to support compliant behaviour. Rather than punish Jack's uncompliant acts, the teacher ignored minor acts but she also ignored some defiant behaviour. The teacher knew that she allowed Jack to manipulate her and monopolise her time, and described herself as 'constantly falling into Jack's trap'. The fact that the teacher described his behaviour as 'Jack's trap' indicated that she perceived Jack to be manipulative rather than impulsive or out of control.

The classroom system supported Jack's maladaptive behaviour by the structure of the behaviour modification programme that aimed to give Jack some control over his behaviour. You may remember that the teacher responded to certain acts of troublesome behaviour by:

- giving at least one warning;
- giving minutes of time out on a minute by minute basis;
- allowing Jack to neutralise the time out minutes when he behaved properly.

These strategies ensured that Jack retained his power to behave in a compliant and uncompliant way *as* he desired and *when* he decided. His use of compliant behaviour at times enabled him to maintain his status with the other children, and his status was added to continually by his teacher's interactions that aimed to support and encourage his achievements. When Jack made a mistake and was not able to neutralise the time-out minutes by lunch time then he resorted to defiance, which on several occasions allowed him to achieve just what he wanted; his lunch-time play.

It seems reasonable to infer that Jack understood how the classroom and school system worked and he used his cognitions to achieve certain goals. The supportive classroom offered no threat to his self-concept and he was a well-liked member of his peer group.

The school context inadvertently provided opportunities for Jack to behave in maladaptive ways. Some aspects of the contexts were supporting Jack to be manipulative and demanding, and it is unlikely that this situation had long-term benefits for Jack or for the other children in his class.

It seemed that Jack's teachers had decided to ignore many of his small acts of disruptive behaviour, however the children did not ignore them and at times they supported it with their laughter. We need to ask how helpful it was for Jack's development to ignore his tendency engage in defiance, which amused his peers and raised his status in their eyes.

It seems that the staff's understanding and acceptance of the ADHD diagnosis precluded them from investigating Jack's behaviour further. Case study material showed that Jack was displaying some traits associated with challenging behaviour problems, which include a lack of impulsive behaviour and defiance directed firstly to the mother. Further analysis of Jack's relationships at school and at home may have helped staff to think through how the context could support Jack to adapt his cognition and emotions in positive ways.

Case study 3 – David

Seven-year-old David lived at home with his mother and father. He had no siblings. He attended year two of his local primary school in a class of 22 children that included a boy confined to a wheelchair with cerebral palsy who had a full-time assistant.

David's mother reported that his birth had been 'very traumatic' and that they both had been very ill for the following 12 months. David had sleep problems and had never developed a regular sleeping pattern. He was judged to be 'hyperactive' before he was two years of age.

His mother reported that before he received medication, David's behaviour was impulsive and placed him in danger. For example, he ran from his house onto a busy road. David's mother said that when he attended pre-primary he was 'extremely aggressive' towards his peers. She had problems with the other children's parents and they told her that the children were frightened of David because of his aggressive behaviour. David was referred for paediatric assessment during the pre-primary year, was diagnosed as having ADHD and prescribed medication.

David's mother and father had attended counselling with a psychiatrist and had completed an in-home behaviour modification programme that involved a psychologist making daily home visits for four months. The aim of the programme was to instruct David's parents in order to help them manage, control and change David's aggressive behaviour. David's mother reported that the medication plus the behaviour programme had helped David, her husband and herself to deal with his impulsive and aggressive behaviour. His mother described David as, 'well-mannered, considerate and loving', and she said that the recent improvements in his behaviour were due to the 'hard work and devotion' of many people. However, she said that although David had made rapid gains, he would need intensive work for several years.

The school principal did not offer any information regarding David's background or family situation, but said that there was regular contact with David's mother. The principal noted that David's class teacher had made 'wonderful progress' with him during the year.

The classroom teacher reported that David's 'mental ability outweighed his physical ability academically' and he was reluctant to attempt tasks when he knew that he could not produce the quality of work that he wanted and expected from himself.

In David's class children selected their own places to sit and were encouraged to make their choice on the basis of a friend with whom they thought they could work well. David had chosen to sit next to the boy with cerebral palsy for two terms, however during the third term he had moved to sit with two other boys, Paul and Anthony.

Teacher–child interactions

Observations showed that David responded appropriately to 58 per cent of the teacher's instructions, and inappropriately to 42 per cent of instructions. However, the teacher tended to ignore David's many inappropriate responses and responded to only 17 per cent of his uncompliant acts. Similarly, the teacher responded to 18 per cent of David's compliant acts. An example of teacher's response to compliance is seen in the following vignette, which took place during group time when the teacher asked children to name characters from a story:

> David looked around the group and did not put his hand up, unlike many other children. He leaned across to James sitting next to him and whispered 'Mrs Potts', then he put his hand up and looked at the class teacher. The teacher smiled as she looked at David and said, 'Who's another character David?' David replied 'Mrs Potts'. The teacher responded with 'Great', and added Mrs Potts to the list on the easel. David watched his teacher with some fingers in his mouth, while he rubbed his eyes with his other hand.

Observations showed that David often did not participate fully during group times, and the teacher was observed to use strategies that encouraged him to join in. The teacher seemed to find ways at group time to communicate with David *indirectly* about what he needed to do and David understood and responded appropriately to the indirect interaction. An example was seen when the class had been nominating their preferred ending to a story:

> The teacher asked, 'Who liked the ending where ...?' David did not put his hand up and continued to look at the teacher as she asked 'Who liked the ending where ...?' David continued to look at the teacher but did not put his hand up. The teacher scanned the group and said that the children who hadn't voted for an ending would need to make up their own ending. David looked at his teacher and nodded.

At times David's contributions during class were accepted even though he transgressed the 'hands up to speak rule'. For example, the teacher asked a question and David responded:

> David put his hand up and the teacher called on him to answer 'Yes David?' David looked at the teacher and said, 'Um. I've forgotten'. The teacher called on another child who also said she'd forgotten. Then David called out 'Now I remember', and the teacher said 'Good. Yes David?'. The teacher enlarged on David's answer and he sat still in his chair with his arms folded on the desk and kept looking as the teacher spoke to the group.

David showed clear understanding about the classroom rules concerning turn-taking at group times:

Interviewer: What do you have to do when the teacher asks the children a question and you want to answer?
David: You have to put your hand up and then the teacher says 'Yes' and then you answer.
Interviewer: Do you always join in at question time?
David: Mmm sometimes I just keep the answer in my head.
Interviewer: Does anyone ever call out answers?

David: Nah. You just put your hand up.

David showed that he knew it was unacceptable to call out or make noises during class, and observations showed that he did this on only three occasions, and the teacher chastised him two out of the three times.

Individual seatwork presented some problems for David who appeared to find it hard to get going and complete set tasks. His teacher was observed to respond quickly to his non-verbal cues but she did not assume information and seemed to encourage David to seek help when he needed it:

> David sat back in his chair and looked across the room to his teacher. She looked at David, pointed to herself and asked, 'Do you want me?' David nodded and smiled as the teacher walked towards him. She crouched in front of his desk and spoke to him about his work. She coached him until he got going again and then said, 'you're going well. Good on you', and patted his head as she walked away. David sat back in his chair and continued to write in his book.

Findings showed that David initiated 54 per cent of all interactions with his teachers and that 80 per cent of David's initiations evoked a positive reaction from them. Observations showed that all the teacher-initiated interactions were positive and included:

- selecting David to participate in activities;
- asking if he was managing his work;
- supporting him with his work.

When David was praised he responded with appropriate behaviour and sustained compliance with the classroom rules. An example was seen during music when he was awarded two stickers for compliant behaviour and later he was asked why he was given them:

David: Oh because Mrs Howard gave me this one when she chose me to be a chimney pot, and this one when she chose me to be in the song.
Interviewer: Why do you think Mrs Howard picked you?
David: Because … I did everything right.
Interviewer: Great. What kinds of things did you do to be chosen?
David: Um. Well I put my hand up to be chosen and I sat nicely, and I think maybe the tablets probably maybe helped me to remember.
Interviewer: Oh.
David: Did you know about the tablets?
Interviewer: No I didn't.
David: Yeah. They help me at school, and to be kind, and concentrate.

Peer interactions

David's interactions with his peers in the classroom were characterised by a range of positive and negative interactions. He was observed to take the lead when cooperation and partner work skills were required. On one occasion the children had been asked to find a partner and stand together:

> David looked around the group and then turned to face Georgia and said, 'I'll be your partner, okay?' Georgia nodded and smiled and moved to stand next to David. Later the children were instructed by the teacher to practice a particular skill with the hoops. David passed his hoop to Georgia and said, 'You go first'. Georgia tossed the two hoops together to David who caught them. Georgia clapped and laughed saying 'Well done'. David put the two hoops together, looked at Georgia and said 'You ready?' then he tossed the hoops to her.

David demonstrated his understanding of sharing materials and equipment in class, for example when he and his partner ran out of blocks and needed more for their construction:

> David said, 'Melanie go and get some more blocks from over there'. Melanie said they weren't allowed to and David walked across the room to Ben and asked, 'Ben, can I please borrow these?' Ben replied 'Any one David'. David smiled and said, 'Oh thanks. You're my best buddy', and took the blocks back to Melanie.

Observations showed that in class David interacted mainly with three boys, Anthony, Mark and Paul, and that the interactions often ended up with negative outcomes for David. This is in the next example which began when David opened his drawer and took out a pencil which had been broken in two.

> David said, 'Hey Anthony look!' and Anthony looked at the pencil and said, 'Yeah' before going back to his work. Paul looked across at the pencil and asked, 'Can I have it?' David nodded, passed over the pencil and leant on his desk with his feet on his chair. Paul passed the pencil to Mark who said, 'It doesn't join properly', and returned it to David. Paul and Mark continued with their work as David looked at the broken pencil. Paul nudged David's arm saying, ' Move it', then he pushed David's arm off his desk. David turned to Ben, and offered him the pencil. Paul leaned across the desk and called 'Say "no" Ben', while David said 'Say "yes"'. Ben looked at the pencil then at David and said, 'Well. I already have three broken pencils so I'll say no'. Paul looked at Ben, smiled and nodded his head. David sat staring at the pencil.

The previous example showed the subtle ways that children include or exclude their peers and the constant negotiations that it involves, however David continued to initiate interactions with the boys. At times David was sent direct negative messages but it appeared that he chose not to respond overtly and seemed instead to 'switch off':

> The teacher had instructed children to work with their neighbour, which meant that Anthony had to work with David. David sat watching the teacher and Anthony spoke slowly through clenched teeth, 'David, I have to be with you. I ... don't ... like ... it!' David did not respond and continued to look at the teacher. Anthony said, 'David! Hello! We're working together!' but David did not acknowledge Anthony's comments and continued to look at the teacher.

In spite of some negative interactions in the classroom, David was observed interacting with Anthony, Mark and Paul in the playground, however he spent considerable periods of time with one friend, Alex. At times the children's games involved considerable rough housing that remained at a low level, for example, shouting, pulling at jumpers and sometimes rolling around on the grass. After one playtime, the interviewer asked David about his games:

David: They were fighting. Like I said we real fight.
Interviewer: And why was Paul chasing you?
David: Mmm because we, I me and my friend Alex and Tyrone have hmmm defeated all my enemies! And they're our new ones!
Interviewer: Mmm because I saw Paul grab the back of your jumper and he was pulling and pulling your arm.
David: Yeah. But then I remembered my star and went rrrhhh into his arm just a little, like this ...
Interviewer: So is it a game that you play?
David: No. It's really serious. And me, Alex and Tyrone always win.

Conversations with David showed that he expressed few constructs about friendship apart from the notion that friends play games together. However, David showed the understanding that friends fight and then make up and he said:

... Alex used to be, I used to be his friend but every time he came over we used to be fighting and everything! ... I always started fighting. Just like pushing and things. I used to be pushing him and that.
Interviewer: And what made you friends then, if you used to fight?
David: Cause then we um, just became friends, because I didn't do it anymore.

The above extract appears to show that David understood his responsibility as a friend and his power to change his behaviour in order to maintain the friendship. When David was shown a picture of a boy who wanted to join a game he said:

David: Ask them.
Interviewer: What could he say?
David: 'Can I please join in with you?'
Interviewer: mmm what do you think these boys might say?
David: 'If you play it very good'.
Interviewer: What if they said 'No'. What else could he do?
David: He would be crying.
Interviewer: Could he do anything else to get them to let him play?
David: No.

David appeared to know that friends want you to play if you play properly, and he seemed to know that he was able to make this choice.

Commentary

The analysis of this case study attempts to identify the adaptations that David was making to the context. The diagnosis of ADHD has not been treated as an individual within-child deficit that could be treated by medication alone. It is significant that David's mother referred to their difficult first twelve months together and the fact that she and David were ill for an extended period of time. We know little of this period and the type of support that was available to the family during this time, but it is possible that the early health problems impacted the development of a secure attachment relationship between David and his mother, who was the primary caregiver.

The medical diagnosis of David's behaviour led to the involvement of a range of experts with the family, and this seems to have resulted in a supportive home context. David's parents had participated in an intensive programme to learn new ways of interacting with their son and managing his behaviour, this indicated that they accept their responsibility as parents for his behaviour. We can infer that the psychologist's visits had enabled David and his parents to develop more appropriate relationships that have established their parent/child roles with greater clarity. His mother appeared to be comfortable with the view that she was not solely responsible for David's behaviour, and neither was she seeking quick fix cures. She commented that he would need expert intervention for an extended period of time and she acknowledged that the efforts of other people have helped David to develop to his current level.

David's home context has supported him to develop the important friendship skills he needs at school. For example, he referred to his friend Alex visiting his house, which indicated that his parents accepted that having friends to play is an important part of childhood. David accepted that he is at least partly responsible for looking after his friendships. He recognised that Alex did not want to play with him when he was not cooperative, which has led him to adapt his behaviour in order to achieve the goal of having a friend.

The classroom was a supportive context that enabled David to continue to adapt strategies to be a fully participating member of the class. David's relationship with his teacher was positive, and they had developed a way of communicating through signals and cues that did not require verbal messages, so that David could convey that he needed help without other children knowing. The teacher was quick to respond to David without creating dependence by expecting him to accept the responsibility of working out when he needed help and seeking it appropriately. The teacher's interactions with David provided an appropriate model for the other members of David's class, and many examples showed that he experienced many positive interactions with his peers throughout his day.

The quality of the relationship between David and his teacher fostered his development in several different areas. Some of David's interactions with a small group of boys ended negatively, but he appeared to be keen to be accepted by the group. In addition, David experienced a great deal of acceptance from other children in his class that provided support for his skills in cooperating with others and being a resourceful person.

David credited his tablets with helping him to be kind and concentrate, but in addition, he showed awareness that he was responsible for his behaviour. Although articulate, David had trouble expressing ideas about friendship, which may indicate his lack of experience or earlier negative experiences. Opportunities to talk about his relationships with peers and adults may help him to further clarify cognitions about his roles and responsibilities in his relationships.

In summary, evidence suggests that David had shifted his modes of adaptation as he responded to the school situation. He had found that his old ways of relating to his peers did not bring him what he wanted, which was to have friends and be part of the group. The supportive contexts of home and school had enabled David to develop cognitions that are likely to help him achieve his goal.

Summary

I have outlined three case studies to highlight the importance of attending to all contexts of children's development in order to change troublesome classroom behaviour. Case studies can provide teachers with a wealth of information about a child, and objective reporting of classroom interactions may reveal aspects of the context previously hidden from view. Case studies have the capacity to reveal the ways in which children adapt to the classroom context and how it shapes their goals of adaptation.

One interpretation of the three cases is that the medical diagnosis of ADHD provided a zone of proximal development for the three children, to a greater or lesser extent. None of the schools had planned behaviour management programmes, presumably because they were confident that medication was sufficient to meet the child's needs. However, current good practice for children diagnosed as ADHD advises that children need behaviour management programmes that incorporate cognitive-behavioural strategies and effective instructional techniques (Reid, Maag, Vase and Wright, 1994).

The schools' acceptance of the medical diagnosis had stopped them from investigating the context to ensure that it was fair and just for all children. Further, schools had not talked to the children about their view of classroom life and what they knew, feared, longed for, or had fantasies about. A strong thread in the field notes was that the friendship and social concerns was the driving force of many interactions, both positive and negative. Many of these interactions were covert with powerful meanings for all the participants.

Children need to have their private lives, and teachers need to balance knowing about the dynamics and respecting children's needs to be autonomous. However, turning a blind eye to victimisation, or worse, being part of victimisation, means abdicating responsibilities to vulnerable children. Duty of care means that schools must know about, monitor and at times take action to prevent injustice in classrooms.

Teachers argue that they don't have time to observe children and document what happens in classrooms and they don't have time to sit around talking with children. However, it is important to ask questions about the time and energy that was invested by Tom's teacher and if it paid good dividends. The negative classroom climate was hardly a pleasant place for Tom, his peers or his teacher, and it was the source of a constant drain on energy and time.

We have to ask if accepting Jack's troublesome behaviour was in his best long-term interest. Further information may have informed teaching staff that Jack's behaviour warranted some different strategies in order to keep him on a developmental pathway that would enable him to achieve his potentials.

I suggest that an intensive period of working with a colleague could result in rich benefits for the classroom. There are several strategies that can help teachers overcome the constraints of time and energy. For example, having a colleague to observe over several days at different times of the day in different situations. Using video or audio-recordings, and asking assistants to record information on a checklist are practical strategies to gain objective information about the classroom. Talking with children about specific incidents and listening carefully to their explanations and reasoning can provoke further thinking on the classroom dynamics. However, it is clear that trust relationships between teacher and child will underpin the success of these strategies.

Chapter 5

Schools and troublesome behaviour

> The school sets the parameter of what's acceptable behaviour ... but the child might be inside that parameter with one teacher and outside it with another.
>
> Primary school principal

In the previous chapters I focused on teachers and children, and outlined ways in which teachers can investigate troublesome behaviours in systematic ways. This chapter looks at school systems and ways in which investigating the school systems might lead to evidence-based practices that support children's appropriate behaviours.

I begin the chapter by taking issue with the idea that teachers should be expected to work as autonomous professionals in managing troublesome behaviours. As the extract at the top of the page indicates, teachers work with colleagues and how they work together to plan and implement school policy can make a great deal of difference to children's behaviour. When children are 'inside the parameters' of acceptable behaviour with one teacher but not another they will receive confused messages that do little to help them learn. I suggest that developing collaborative relationships is a key strategy that can make a difference to children's troublesome behaviour and that the school principal has a pivotal role in facilitating collaboration.

Schools and relationships

Relationships in schools are complex because they involve covert power relations. Issues of power may hinder schools from establishing more equitable ways of working that ensure the best guidance for children with troublesome behaviours. Schools may find it difficult to change accepted practices when there is a hierarchal division of power with the principal at the top and staff in subordinate roles (Sarup, 1982).

Teachers who feel empowered are able to ask questions, raise issues and confront knowledge that is unjust and oppressive, and to use their understandings to guide change processes (MacNaughton and Williams, 1998). However, it may be difficult for junior staff to speak up about injustice particularly when they have little security of employment. Constructing ways for all staff to have opportunities to raise issues without fear of reprisal is one way that schools can make sure that the management systems create a just context for all teachers and children.

School leaders may assume that the school provides teachers with equal opportunities to achieve success as professionals, however this basic assumption allows issues to remain hidden. Fair and just contexts can facilitate opportunities for teachers to flourish by addressing false perceptions, expectations, labelling and stereotyping that diminish competence (MacNaughton and Williams, 1998). Staff can address issues when they have open discussions in trust relationships with their colleagues, but one barrier is the norm of individualism found in some school systems.

A decade ago, researchers found that teachers were isolated in the 'secret garden' of their classrooms and that schools perpetuated ideas about teachers' autonomy and privacy (Little, 1990). It seems that teachers wanted to keep themselves safe from criticism by closing the classroom door, but at the same time, they felt lonely and helpless to deal with troublesome behaviour and classroom management. One reason why individualism has been strong in schools is the belief that teachers should be able to 'do it alone' because they are autonomous professionals. But teachers' sense of autonomy may be an illusion that promotes a false sense of empowerment (Ball, 1987).

Research has shown that teachers who worked in schools where collaborative practice was the norm found that they had help to understand more about classroom dynamics or to work together to design creative strategies to help children behave appropriately. They worked in schools where making mistakes was seen as a way to develop different teaching strategies or analyse school systems with a view to improvement (Little, 1990).

After many years of saying that schools would benefit from collaborative practice, a recent study found that participants worked in school contexts where staff worked alone with little collegial contact (Corrie, 2000). The newly qualified teachers (NQTs) in these schools felt unable to share their difficulties because they feared that their colleagues would judge them as being incompetent at the job of teaching.

Many teachers remember their first year of teaching vividly, which has a great impact on practitioners and shapes their practices in countless ways. The beginning years influence teachers' values, expectations and beliefs about the profession. Here I report the experiences of a group of NQTs who had taken part in a special programme to foster collaborative and reflective skills as undergraduates, and they continued to meet as a group in their first year of teaching. The aim of the support group was to share the joys and woes of the first year of teaching, to continue the reflective process and to work together to solve problems.

I hope the NQTs' stories will help you to understand how their experiences in schools influenced what they knew and did in powerful ways. These teachers' stories may prompt you to reflect on the social justice issues that shape your professional life and the lives of your teaching colleagues, and influence the school's responses to children's troublesome behaviour.

Teachers as collaborative colleagues

Kate's story

Kate was an NQT who worked in a school where the principal was committed to collaborative learning and where all staff were seen as learners able to enhance their skills and knowledge. Right from the start of the school year Kate felt able to seek advice from the other teachers. She said:

> ... I can always go there and say, 'Look, Hammond just isn't doing well, there's something that's just not clicking.' I can really relate to them well, and they give me such good feedback.

The principal fostered the idea that all teachers need to learn from one another and Kate adopted the norm quickly. She reported that she had an appointment with the principal to review her progress:

> He asked me what I had learnt this term and I told him ...

The principal's question helped the teachers to construct themselves as life-long learners and there was no implication that Kate was inefficient because she was learning new things. Kate was not singled out as a learner because all the staff were seen as being on a learning journey that was supported by their colleagues. Kate explained:

> I mean you need that sort of, what is it? We call it the 'collegial support' of those around you.

At the end of her first year, Kate said that being a teacher was like being a rose:

> ... you see the bud of the rose as it comes out, and it is small and it is really tight knit and it continues to grow and it spreads; it has thorns and sometimes they are not very nice and you have to pick them off, if you don't they get bigger and they hurt even more ... ultimately there is great beauty in a rose ... but there are hard things that go with it as well. I wilt very quickly if I don't get lots of feeding ... at times I have wilted because I haven't had enough coming into me. It's not so much support,

> but just, more knowledge, learning, and just time even to do things ... I have had to deal with my own attitudes to kids or parents or other things like that.

Kate's metaphor of a rose showed that she acknowledged that, even with support, teaching was full of challenges. The collaborative school culture had helped her learn more about teaching and more about her own values, and it had enabled her to recognise that, 'there is great beauty in a rose.'

Teachers as individuals

Mary's story

Mary was an NQT who worked in a unit that was located a short distance away from the main site of her school. She attended the school regularly for staff meetings and social events with the staff of 15. Towards the end of the first term she told the support group that she had bumped into the principal that day in the staff room and he had not been able to remember her name.

The head teacher's failure to recall Mary's name conveyed powerful messages to her at a time when she was trying to establish herself as a member of the teaching staff. Mary felt that she was unimportant and what she was striving to achieve was unimportant to the school. She contributed a great deal of energy and enthusiasm to her teaching but got little recognition from the school and no affirmation about her professional status.

The fact that the principal left Mary 'to get on with it alone' meant that she had a great deal of freedom and autonomy, which she enjoyed. It seemed to Mary that nobody in the school knew what she did in her classroom, and as long as there were no complaints, then the principal was happy not to be bothered. However, she had to make decisions and take actions that were difficult without guidance from an experienced educator, and she felt that she had to plead for any help or assistance.

An example of lack of support arose when Mary became concerned about a child's behaviour and suspected that physical abuse was a factor. She documented possible signs of abuse and kept objective anecdotal records for several weeks. One day the child arrived with bruising and disclosed information to her. Mary judged this to be a crisis situation and was very concerned. Immediately she rang the principal to ask for an appointment after school but she found that he was reluctant to wait to see her:

> I said, 'This is important, this child has disclosed this information.' But no, no, if I hadn't been up there at three o'clock: Off! I can feel the bitumen burning as he leaves! ... It's hilarious. No, it's not, it's quite sad ...

By the end of her first year of teaching, Mary said she felt isolated and had given up the idea that collaborative practice was workable in schools. Mary found it hard to share at any level with the members of the support group, who were people she knew well and had collaborated with closely as an undergraduate. It seemed that Mary lost her belief in collaborative relationships, and this was replaced with the view that now she was a teacher she had to work alone.

Denise's story

Mary's experience was not unique. Other NQTs reported stories of professional isolation. In the early weeks of settling down, Denise said that she didn't have much to do with the school staff either. After 16 weeks Denise said that she felt isolated and added:

> There's no opportunity to talk to someone and get the feedback, and to say, 'I'm having these problems', and they say, 'That's OK'. It's hard.

At 26 weeks, Denise had experienced some problems with the children and their parents, and she reiterated that she had no other professional with whom to share her difficulties. She said:

> You're like, just there, on your own; get on with it!

She indicated that she was beginning to accept that teaching was about individual struggle rather than collaborative problem solving. She began to think that collaboration was talked about at university but was not part of the teachers' worlds. Throughout the year, Denise experienced difficulties with the parents and she described them as 'odd people'. At one stage the parents complained to the school principal, Denise reported to the group that the principal said:

> Well just leave it to me and I'll sort it out.

The principal excluded Denise from the negotiations with the parents and thus did not help her learn more about this important aspect of her professional work. Denise was not encouraged to talk to her colleagues about her difficulties, observe in more experienced peers' classrooms, or seek external help. The isolation that Denise experienced did little to help her reflect on, or change her practice. At the end of the year she still experienced problems with the parents and did not know why.

Ann's story

Ann and Denise shared similar experiences but Ann said that she felt she could not seek guidance from other staff members because:

> You feel as if everybody is ... looking after their own patch, they are all busy with their own little bit.

Ann's school being 'too busy' provided a rationale for lack of collaboration. Ann was experienced in collaborative practice, and she was surprised by the lack of colleagiality. Half way through her year, she commented:

> I really miss this opportunity (to collaborate) – most of my colleagues are either very traditional or too afraid to do things differently, I find this extremely frustrating. I try to discuss ideas with several other staff members but this is not very satisfying.

Gradually Ann became silenced in a school culture that she felt powerless to change. She adapted to the culture of individualism by not expecting to collaborate with her colleagues.

Lee's story

Lee was one of the NQTs who experienced problems with classroom management but did not feel able to share her concerns with other staff. Lee had been thrilled to get her first appointment half way through the year, but she soon realised that she had been assigned the 'worst class in the school'. The difficulties with the class were well known in the school and had caused the previous teacher to resign. Lee, the newcomer, had been given the class with no help or guidance from the principal or senior staff, and soon found herself floundering. However, she was reluctant to seek advice and was scared that somebody would find out about her difficulties:

> I'm more scared about the noise level. All they have are those fold-away doors between the classrooms. I made sure they were shut and our door into the middle area was shut. I asked the teacher next door if they could hear us, but no ... (said in a relieved tone of voice).

Lee was not offered any opportunities to learn from more experienced colleagues. The norm of privacy perpetuated the myth that NQTs should have the skills to cope alone, which reinforced the need for Lee to keep the problem a secret. Closed classroom doors symbolised the culture that pervaded the school, this did little to foster a climate of mutual support or help for the least experience colleague.

Lee's difficulties didn't go away and escalated to the point that the principal received some complaints from parents. The principal responded by sending Lee to work in the library for part of the day while a more experienced colleague took the class. No opportunity was given for Lee to talk about the difficulties, to receive support in the classroom or develop the skills needed to manage the class. Lee's confidence plummeted and by the end of the year she was wondering if teaching was the right career choice. She said that:

> ... teaching is like having a room full of keys, turning each one and nothing is working. Each day I walk into the classroom having great expectations, 'I've got this plan and this plan.' I walk out of the classroom each day saying, 'What am I doing?' I go to school with a smile on my face and come home and it's an upside down smile, eyes are droopy.

How do you respond to Lee's story? Do you think a newly qualified teacher should be able to manage alone?

Consider the principal's response. Do you support the principal's decision? If not, how would you help Lee?

Is it less professional to seek help? Or is it less professional to keep problems a personal matter?

Consider Lee's story from a justice viewpoint. Do you think that Lee was treated in a fair and just way?

Is it possible that schools transgress justice issues concerning staff and students?

If you agree, then consider the implications for managing children's behaviour.

In Lee's case, a keen and energetic member of the teaching profession was left to flounder without support. Undoubtedly the principal made decisions that fitted his/her value system. It seems reasonable to infer that Lee's principal, like the principals at Mary and Denise's schools, subscribed to value of individualism and the idea that teachers need to 'go it alone'. It is a common belief that newly qualified teachers need to prove themselves as professionals who cope by themselves. However, this belief did nothing to help Lee understand the children's behaviour and work through approaches that could be helpful in changing the classroom dynamics.

The hands-off strategy of some principals suggests that they thought teachers should enter the profession with the requisite skills to manage the classroom. However, another view is that teachers engage in life-long learning to refine their skills and update their knowledge.

In the last section you read about two newly qualified teachers' images of teaching. Lee's image was like having a bunch of keys and finding that none fit the door so that experiencing success as a teacher was out of her reach.

Kate's image was a beautiful rose. What is your image or metaphor for teaching? Try completing the sentence:

Being a teacher is like ... or

Teaching is like ...

Write down the first image that comes to your mind, without judging it, because it will be the most powerful and truest one for you. What can you learn about your image of teaching? You will learn more about yourself if you do this exercise with colleagues.

Understanding the systems model means recognising that teachers are neither autonomous individuals who do whatever they like in schools, nor are they helpless pawns that cannot exert influence on the school. Teachers are part of the school system and have relationships with the system, which means they interact and stimulate a flow of ideas, values and knowledge between them.

Individual personalities

In telling the stories of the NQTs, it is important to note that these teachers were different people with individual personalities, motivations, knowledge and experiences that influenced their practice. I do not want to imply that these NQTs were helpless victims who were unable to make a difference to their contexts. It is clear that their personalities, skills and competencies made a difference to the ways in which they became part of the school context.

We know that personality traits predispose individuals to behave in particular ways. Researchers investigating babies' behaviours have measured clear differences between infants from day one. For example, some babies are wrigglers, who fidget and fuss; others are still and placid types, and some personality types last a lifetime (Berger and Thompson, 1996). Teachers' personalities lead them to behave in particular ways in schools that influence the outcomes they experience.

In addition to personality, teachers come from a wide range of racial, ethnic, spiritual, experiential and education backgrounds and are at different ages and stages of their teaching careers. Teachers may well have different levels of skills and competencies but judgements about teachers may be made on the basis of fixed attributes. For example:

- 'She's just one of those very quiet people who can't assert themselves ...';
- 'I'm afraid he has a very domineering personality';
- 'She tries hard but just hasn't got any charisma'.

These statements imply that there is nothing that can change a teacher's practice. A more positive view is that teachers can be helped to think through issues with a view to clarifying meanings and changing their practice. Teachers can change their practice when the context facilitates their development. Many teachers are life-long learners who continually add to, or change, their understandings and skills, and they work in schools that provoke and support their growth.

Schools that avoid judging teachers' competencies on the basis of an individual's personality, training or experience are more likely to accept responsibility for teacher development and to examine the ways in which the context might contribute to the teacher's actions. Some schools accept responsibility for teacher growth and engage with the teacher to construct creative solutions, assess school management practices, facilitate the school's work with families or provide a mentor to help the teacher to develop new understandings. Important aspects of the school culture are revealed through the ways that management practices support teachers and assist them to deepen learning.

School culture: 'the way we do things'

It's been widely accepted that what we know occurs through socially constructing knowledge. In other words, we know by talking with others and by sharing views, opinions and questions. The process occurs between school staff because humans are social beings and most people have an inherent desire to be accepted and belong to the group.

Informed by Vygotsky's theory, researchers agree that mental processes occur between people rather than within the individual, which means that mental processes are embedded in social relationships. Cognitive processing, memory and attention enable participants to construct shared meanings about the school culture that is embedded in practice (Wertsch and Tulviste, 1998, p. 14).

Talking with others leads to new ways of thinking, which is an important process at work for teachers when they begin at a new school. Many formal and informal interactions help new staff members learn quickly about the knowledge that is valued in a school. They learn both to adapt to the school culture and make a difference to shared meanings through collaborative practice (Menter, 1995). Generally, new teachers have to fit in to the school culture, and many adopt practices or views that they thought were odd at first.

You may find it helps to clarify your thoughts by stopping at this point and thinking about your current teaching situation or a school you've experienced.

Think about:

- the values that are assumed by the staff. For example, it was accepted by one staff group that the principal was responsible for policy decisions;
- the values or policies that staff debate. For example, policies might be based on the assumption that everyone agrees that 'time out' is an appropriate response to troublesome behaviour but it is not debated and therefore different opinions are not heard;
- how school policies are formed. Where do policies come from? How much staff participation is there? Is it pseudo-collaboration or can staff actually make a difference to policies?
- some of the unwritten rules that govern staff decisions. For example, there may be an unwritten rule that staff should be competent to manage their own classrooms, which would stop staff from seeking help.

School cultures affect teachers in many different ways. Often student teachers comment that during their field experience they adapted quickly to the attitudes and values being expressed by experienced staff members, even though fundamentally they clashed with their own knowledge. Some student teachers are shocked at how rapidly this process happened, and they say that they were surprised to hear themselves *sounding* like their supervising teacher, even though his/her practice did not match their ideal.

Teachers have to fit in to the school, this paves the way for them to accept the school's knowledge about children, teaching and learning, and the possibilities in a particular school context (Kuzmic, 1993; Menter, 1995). Experienced teachers who find the school culture is alien may withdraw physically by leaving the school, or psychologically by distancing themselves from the staff (Corrie, 1997).

Before you continue reading, think about the previous section. Try to recall and write about a time when you felt that your colleagues supported you.

Have you ever worked with a colleague or colleagues with whom you could go and share problems? If not, try and work out why you did not seek help from a colleague.

Did you trust your colleague to help you work through a difficult situation? Did you worry that they would think less of you as a professional?

If you have, write about it. If not, write about how you feel about not having a teaching colleague to turn to for help.

Do you want to work in a collaborative school culture? Why or why not? These reflections may help make your beliefs clear to you.

Teachers who work in collaborative school cultures develop good working relationships with colleagues who they can turn to when the going gets tough. They are able to go to other teachers and talk openly and honestly about their difficulties. In some schools, colleagues visit their classrooms and give feedback, which is used to plan intervention and changes.

Norms are established quickly and reinforced every day in schools. Teachers may experience collaborative relationships that shape staff dynamics and lead to approaches to classroom management. Collaborative practice becomes a frame of reference to judge many situations (Nias, 1985).

It would be useful for you to stop reading at this point and reflect on the school and education system you know about or have experienced. Is staff individualism or collaboration most prominent?

On a scale of one to ten, where one is 'most individual' and ten 'most collaborative' how would you rate your experiences?

How have your experiences influenced your expectations about classroom practice?

You may consider if you would prefer to be in a group of collaborative colleagues or individuals, and why.

If you agree that collaboration is useful, suggest how it could be fostered in your school.

Collaboration can help teachers draw on a range of expertise with a view to creating their responses to difficult situations with children's behaviour.

School leaders

The leadership of a school setting has a crucial role to play in relationships that develop. In some schools, staff are sustained by collaborative relationships that provides them a great deal of support (Corrie, 1993). School leaders subtly influence many aspects of school life, and influence teachers' sense of job satisfaction, professional fulfilment, and their approaches to classroom behaviour.

The principal and other experienced members of the power hierarchy influence the knowledge that is constructed in the school. Aspects of the school culture may be shown when principals explain their reasons and beliefs for events. For example, when two principals were asked why they thought some children had troublesome classroom behaviour, one said:

> I think ... the family perceives education in a different way: either they're not very positive about education, so the children coming in don't have

> an idea of education, as such, and they find school is a bit of a bore ... or children are coming from families that seem to have a history of dropping out of school very early and education is perceived as a way of getting rid of children for the day.

The second principal said:

> I think there's a whole lot of things. You've got to look at what the child's ability is, and whether, in fact, what's on offer is suited to that child's learning needs.

The principals' beliefs shaped the way staff viewed and responded to children's troublesome behaviour. The two schools approached children's troublesome behaviour in different ways that reflected what was known about the parents, and new staff quickly reshaped their own knowledge to fit the school culture.

Social justice at the school level may contribute to teachers' management of children's troublesome behaviour in covert ways. The following scenarios show how the decisions of the school leadership can create barriers to teachers' successful outcomes.

- A principal was slow to implement processes to organise an assistant for a child with challenging special needs and the teacher had to manage alone in the classroom. The teacher felt anxious about the amount of his time that was being taken up with one child, and other children began to act with increasingly troublesome behaviours.
- A principal believed that possible sexual abuse should be left to other professionals to follow up. The principal ignored the teacher's reports of persistent indicators of concern seen in the child's troublesome behaviour. The teacher felt helpless to act and angry about the lack of support.
- The deputy principal allocated classes for the new school year and gave herself the most desirable group. She assigned the class with the worst reputation to the least-experienced teacher. The children quickly responded with escalating degrees of troublesome behaviour and eventually parents complained to the principal.
- The specialist teacher was given a classroom that resembled a broom closet because she attended the school only two days a week to give extra tuition in literacy. The inadequate physical resources created problems for the teacher who had to resort to worksheets and individual work to control children. However, the children became uncompliant and unresponsive.

As can be seen in these scenarios, school-level decisions can provide opportunities for troublesome behaviours to escalate, which can occur when teachers get harassed and vulnerable children feel stressed. A system's perspective can help schools to look at all the elements that may influence the behaviours, rather than wondering what's wrong with the child.

The principal has the power to foster collaborative relationships but must believe that collaboration is worth the time and effort. Principals who believe that collaborative relationships will enhance school development ensure that resources are committed to the process, for example, by giving staff non-teaching time to meet together to talk about their teaching, to visit classrooms, to conduct peer observations or assist in data gathering for action research.

Some principals have sought to implement a 'whole school' approach to manage troublesome behaviour. Whole school policies endeavour to ensure that children experience a cohesive and systematic approach to managing behaviour. But teachers influence the system in many covert and overt ways. For instance, one principal developed a new policy to deal with children's inappropriate playground behaviour and sent a note to the staff explaining the procedures they had to follow. Some staff didn't like the idea and so they looked the other way when they were on playground duty, or they implemented part of the policy but not all the steps. When questions were raised they claimed to have forgotten or to have misunderstood the procedures. Eventually the policy just faded away and everybody breathed a sigh of relief, although the playground behaviours still caused difficulties for staff and children.

The whole school approach is more helpful than fragmented and individual teacher strategies, but it is not a panacea. Schools may realise that whole school approaches require effort and time to design, implement and monitor. Staff might be persuaded that what they need is a 'discipline package' in their school because the hard work of design has been done for them. The following section examines the problems inherent in commercial discipline packages as a whole school solution and explains why they are unlikely to change the situation in the long term.

Discipline packages

At the same time as teachers have experienced increases in troublesome behaviours, changes in education systems have resulted in fewer personnel to offer expert guidance to teachers. It is not surprising that some educators respond to the lack of specialist support by turning to commercial enterprise that offers 'quick and easy' solutions to troublesome behaviours.

Commercial discipline packages are sold to schools, usually with workshops for teachers to become trained in the use of the package. Schools buy in the discipline package, which seem to be a good idea, as the creators of the packages have tested the strategies and assert that they work effectively. The steps to achieve positive changes to children's behaviour have been identified and all the school has to do it to follow the guide. A key to success is that the whole school is involved in the programme to ensure consistency between staff members. Teachers have to follow the prescribed instructions and implement predictable consequences for inappropriate behaviour, known to children and staff alike.

At the surface level, it may seem these packages are treating the school as a system and that they help schools to provide a consistent response to children's behaviour. Unfortunately research shows that managing children's behaviour is not as easy as buying a package (Watkins and Wagner, 2000).

Often the use of the discipline packages follows a similar pattern:

1 First, teachers were keen on the package because they thought it was the solution to behaviour problems. In the beginning they followed the programme guidelines carefully and their enthusiasm for the programme increased when they started noticing changes in children's behaviour.
2 After a while the teachers observed that the programme wasn't working so well any more, and that changes in children's behaviour were wearing off.
3 Teachers responded by changing some elements of the programme, and sometimes these changes were based on individual teachers' decisions. Gradually the programme got less and less like the original.
4 In time, teachers moved from the school and the staff group changed. Some of the teachers who had wanted the programme, believed in it and supported it, were no longer in the school, and the new staff group decided to leave the programme up to individuals and its use faded out. Teachers commented that, 'It's probably a good programme, but it just wasn't right for *our* school.'

Researchers have identified several reasons why commercial packages are not likely to help change children's troublesome behaviour in the long-term (Nicholls and Houghton, 1995). One reason is that although the packages seem good – being aimed at the whole school context – they are decontextualised remedies that have not been tailored for a specific school or group of children. A programme may be constructed for one population, such as children who attend North American inner-city schools, and trials are conducted with that group, and possibly other similar groups. It is found to be successful and the creators of the package promote it as a good example of a package that changes children's behaviour.

The package is then sold to educators in another country where the sociocultural context is different and people have different beliefs, values and expectations. Difficulties with these programmes occur at many different levels that reflect their context of origin, and they can shape relationships in ways that seem false to teachers. For example, a programme may direct teachers to use particular words or phrases when dealing with children's behaviour, but they are not the teachers' words and don't fit their way of interacting. In addition, prescriptive programmes tend to promote 'sheer compliance' rather than encouraging children to make choices based on reasoned decisions, which is at odds with active learning approaches (McCaslin and Good, 1998).

Often teachers experience discomfort due to a clash between their values and the values of the programme. They find it is easy to let the programme go or make gradual changes until the package bears little resemblance to the original. New research has shown the importance of context, and it has helped educators understand the problems of using materials out of the contexts for which it was developed.

Many commercial packages have been properly validated with particular groups of children, but teachers cannot assume that all materials that are sold to schools have been subjected to scientific trials. Teachers must be aware that some whole school commercial programmes promote strategies using dubious techniques that are unsubstantiated by research. For example, new interest in brain research has occurred at the same time as commercial materials are being promoted in schools. Some materials claim to be based on the new brain research, and claim to help children behave properly and learn without difficulty. The packages often include specific physical exercises and the promoters infer that the exercises will change children's brain patterns and make them attentive, amenable and eager to learn.

These packages would provide a great deal of benefit if children's behaviour could be changed so easily. But a wealth of research shows that there is little evidence to support the claims, and indeed these packages have little effect on children's behaviour (Kavale and Mattson, 1983; National Health and Medical Research Council, 1997; Silver, 1995).

Similarly, schools may use 'off the shelf' curricula to teach social skills, social problem-solving or conflict resolution skills, but many have not been evaluated properly and have demonstrated limited results that fade quickly (Van-Acker and Talbott, 1999). Teachers need to think critically when presented with programmes that claim to reduce disruptive classroom behaviour, and they need to treat the quick and easy fixes with great caution. Teachers are urged to press for research evidence to support the claims made by people promoting particular programmes, and they have every reason to be cautious about claims that are, 'vague, outdated, metaphorical, or based on misconceptions' (Bruer, 1998, p. 9).

Teachers show their professionalism when they question innovations being sold to schools. In particular, teachers are wise to consider the type of pedagogy (ways of teaching and learning) and values inherent in a particular approach. Watkins and Wagner (2000, p. 48) point out that packages may encourage teachers to react to events and follow a prescribed set of responses rather than planning classrooms that allow all children to learn. Schools are likely to find investigating children's behaviour in systematic ways will help them plan more effective strategies than can be offered by commercial programmes.

Spend some time now thinking about the school context where you work, or one that you know.

Does the school use a whole-school approach to discipline?
If not, why not?

If it is not a commercial package, who designed it?

What are the strengths of the approach?
What aspects need strengthening?

If the school does use a whole-school approach, is it part of a commercial package?

Think about the steps that teachers take to implement the discipline programme:

- list the aspects of the programme that work well;
- list the aspects of the programme that don't work well;
- outline why you think the programme works or doesn't work well.

Schools that design their own whole school approach to discipline through ongoing staff collaboration are likely to manage children's behaviour successfully. Whole school approaches are unlikely to work in the long term when they are bought in, or designed by the senior management and imposed on teachers. Neither commercial packages nor programmes designed by senior management reflect a collaborative approach to children's troublesome behaviour. Building collaborative practice takes time and requires certain values to be deeply embedded in the school culture. The following section outlines some strategies that may foster collaboration.

Building collaborative practice

There are several reasons to foster collaborative practice that include:

- changes to curriculum and assessment in many school systems require collaborative relationships to enable staff to work through the change process in supportive ways;
- schools are expected to collaborate with parents in order to engage them as partners in their children's education;
- schools need to collaborate with a wide range of professionals providing medical and social welfare services to rising numbers of high-risk children;
- school-based management has led to a whole range of additional roles and responsibilities for school staff and collaboration is one way to cope with the changes.

A first step in the collaborative process is to create opportunities to establish common meanings or identify differences between colleagues. It is easy for staff to believe that everybody in the school thinks the same way about children's behaviour, but when they sit down to talk about their meanings they find that there are important differences. For example, when primary school teachers were asked to give their views on the importance of rules in the classroom they said that everybody on their school staff thought the same way about the importance of rules. But when they were asked to explain their meanings they gave very different definitions, and they had different ideas about classroom management. There was no agreement across the staff because ideas had been interpreted in many different ways, which meant that teachers' practices varied a great deal (Corrie, 1993).

Staff may assume that they all think the same way about children's behaviour and that they don't need to spend time talking about their meanings and interpretations. Teachers are more inclined to want to find solutions to problems rather than talk about their meanings. However, differences and taken for granted assumptions about behaviour are revealed when teachers discuss their views openly in a spirit of trust. Talking seriously and deeply about children is one way to challenge, and perhaps change, the status quo in a school.

Talking to colleagues about children and classroom management can help teachers to clarify contradictions that inadvertently may prevent them from achieving their goals. Talking to others can help reduce feelings of isolation and helplessness, and simply hearing oneself say the words aloud to another person can change ideas about a situation.

Increasingly schools have embraced the idea of collaboration, although they may be at different stages of building a collaborative culture. Elements that can be identified in collaborative school cultures include:

An open door policy
Teachers welcome visitors to their rooms, including colleagues, other professionals or children's parents. Colleagues visit their peers to observe and give feedback or to learn new strategies and approaches. Colleagues drop in to classrooms to support teachers or seek help without fear of criticism or intrusion. Open doors encourage frequent interaction that allows understanding and trust to develop.

The principal and senior management model collaboration
Senior staff are available for informal conversations as well as formal meetings. Senior staff respect the views of all staff and seek them out. Teachers feel able to share openly and honestly with the principal and senior staff without fear of being judged as incompetent. A culture of trust and professionalism underpins school practice. Parents and families

are treated as partners in their child's education and their views are treated with respect.

Staff as learners

Principals who show that they believe in and engage in life-long professional development provide a good role model for teachers. Principals can help perpetuate this norm by reviewing the progress of the school and 'what we have learnt this term' as the staff complete special projects or participate in staff development seminars. Care is taken to identify problems as they arise, to analyse them and construct creative solutions.

A warm and welcoming staff room

Key principles of the school culture are enacted informally in the staff room at different times in the day. The staff room is a place where colleagues gather to talk informally about their day, to exchange ideas, share resources, and talk about their learning through seminars, further study courses or professional reading. Staff share their stories of triumphs and disasters without fear of being judged. Colleagues celebrate birthdays and family events and the principal models caring for colleagues as people and professionals. The staff room is maintained carefully as a comfortable and pleasant space that is aesthetically pleasing with pleasant colours, textures, flowers and greenery.

Time for staff to talk to one another

The principal allocates time for teachers to talk deeply and seriously about their work, with a view to supporting one another in their change process. Staff have time allocated for observing in their colleagues' rooms and giving honest feedback. Staff collaborate to collect data about their classrooms in systematic ways to open up discussions further. Staff collaborate to collect data about the whole school context, for example, what happens in the playground, canteen, library and art room, in order to reflect on the patterns in behaviour and events and plan changes if necessary.

Recognition of skills, talents and achievements

The principal gives public recognition for activities that spread the word that teachers are learners and that teachers are competent and highly regarded professionals. Success and achievements are celebrated and used to foster esteem for staff, which is conveyed to the children and parents through different school strategies such as newsletters that are sent home, formal gatherings such as school assemblies and informal contacts with parents.

> *A whole-school policy for behaviour*
> Policies are constructed jointly by school staff and reviewed at regular intervals. Data are gathered from all the stakeholders, which includes parents and children and focus on what works, what doesn't work and how can we do it better. Data are analysed to identify themes and draw valid conclusions that can stimulate reflection and change.
>
> (Corrie, 1993)

I suggest that the research strategy called the 'appreciative inquiry', which is outlined in chapter six, is a suitable approach for investigating the school system and gathering data from a range of stakeholders. The appreciative inquiry can help parents, children and staff focus on positives in the school and how to work together to have more of what they like. Asking parents and children's opinions can provide teachers with insights into difficulties and lead to creative solutions.

Behaviour problems do not disappear when teachers work in collaborative school cultures but they become more manageable. Teachers find that support from colleagues takes the stress away from going it alone. Collaboration enables teachers to gain confidence in their capacity to cope and become objective in their planning to change the situation.

Collaboration can empower teachers by giving them more choice in their professional decisions; this has the capacity to foster social justice (MacNaughton and Williams, 1998). Teachers may be more open to change when they talk at a deep level to their colleagues about what they can change. Collaborative practice can lead teachers to develop ways to ensure that all children have opportunities to enjoy school, learn, have friends, build on their competencies and achieve their potentials.

When teachers make their implicit knowledge *explicit* by talking about it, they may find that they want to change aspects of their practice because there are contradictions between what they know, what they do, and how they want to teach. Staff groups who talk together about what they collectively know about their work find they gain insights into school practices that influence teachers' actions and children's behaviour.

Summary

In this chapter I have looked at some issues at the level of the school system that affect the ways in which schools look at and understand children's troublesome behaviours. I have suggested that schools may reinforce injustice in subtle ways that shape classroom practice, for example, by providing teachers with little opportunity to collaborate with more experienced colleagues. Isolation in a culture of individualism does little to help a teacher who is experiencing difficulties with classroom management.

A collaborative school culture is not a panacea but it can help schools to see where practices can prevent teachers achieving their aims for children. School leaders can take positive steps to ensure that a collaborative culture enhances the professionalism of teachers and fosters social justice for all.

Chapter 6

The teacher-researcher

Investigating troublesome behaviour

In this chapter I ask you to think about expanding your teaching roles in order to include teacher-researcher as part of your work. I explain how research can help you to understand troublesome behaviour and outline some tools that will enable you to explore your own classroom systems.

You may be relieved to know that classroom-based action research does not mean testing children or doing statistical calculations necessarily. Some teachers may enjoy using standardised tests, and quantitative data can be useful. But there are many research techniques that do not require that type of approach and I have introduced some to you already in this book. Teachers can use familiar skills such as systematic and objective observations to investigate troublesome behaviours and this chapter guides you through some steps to take. In addition, it outlines an approach called the 'appreciative inquiry', which can help teachers gain insights into classroom or school systems.

Why research?

Why am I asking teachers to become teacher-researchers? Teacher-researchers have skills to observe and analyse their classroom or school contexts, which empowers them to make their *own* decisions about the types of changes they want to implement. In addition, they act as competent professionals by providing scientific research data to support their decision making. Teachers who base their strategies on research evidence are able to be powerful advocates for the rights of children.

In this book I am urging you to consider being professionals who implement evidence-based practice, and there are important issues of social justice at stake. The findings of classroom-based action research projects can reveal many aspects of classroom life that could remain hidden from view. Hidden elements may foster injustice and making a child conform to inequity can violate basic human rights. Teachers have little power to change a child's home life, but they have a great deal of influence over a classroom or school context.

Social justice can be eroded when teachers assume things about children without making sure that their hunches are right. Plenty of research has shown us how easily teachers' judgements are influenced by their feelings about a child. Often teachers have good intuitions, but sometimes bias and stereotypes increase negative feelings and lead to poor relationships. At the same time, children's behaviours shape what teachers know and feel, but teachers have a professional responsibility to take action and initiate change. However, teachers cannot act from their best guess and they need accurate and objective evidence if they are to make changes that will lead to better learning relationships in classroom and school communities.

Why would teachers decide to learn about and use research strategies rather than asking other professionals, such as an educational psychologist, to visit the classroom and provide solutions to problems? There are many times when teachers need the services of specialists and they should never hesitate to seek out assistance. However, specialist services have been reduced in many education systems and teachers may be disappointed in the results of asking for outside specialist help.

Often teachers need to take action quickly at the beginning of the school year and they can't afford to waste months waiting for an answer from a specialist. In addition, specialists can often provide the best service to the teacher when they have accurate and detailed information about the child or classroom.

Research techniques can help the teacher to gather the information in order to consult with the outside professional about different courses of action. A productive consultation is possible when the teacher presents an array of objective data about the problem. Often the specialist is able to affirm the teacher's actions because the evidence shows that they are doing all the right things.

The advantages of consulting specialists include:

- the teacher can talk about the difficulty and in the process get clear about the issues;
- the teacher can talk about their ideas to help the child and get the specialist's feedback on them;
- the specialist can ask the teacher questions to help her/him develop ideas further;
- the specialist can affirm the teacher's approaches;
- the specialist can provide support and encouragement to the teacher;
- Specialists can use their expert knowledge to develop a programme collaboratively with the teacher.

Sometimes teachers pin their hopes on the expert to tell them exactly what to do to solve the problem. But in some cases the specialist will not be able to offer the teacher appropriate help for a variety of reasons:

1 specialists do not have the classroom teacher's insider knowledge of the context, and therefore they may not have the insights that they may need to illuminate a particular problem;
2 in some school systems, professionals such as educational psychologists, are over-worked and teachers wait for a long time before getting an appointment. Then, because of the pressure of work, the specialist often can only attend a classroom for a short period of time, which does not allow them to make the detailed observations they may require. At times, work pressures prevent the specialist making follow-up visits and the teacher is left to battle on alone;
3 the solutions that outside specialists can offer are likely to be recommended techniques that have worked with teachers and children in different contexts but they might not necessarily be suited to a particular teacher or group of children.

The fact is that teachers are *the experts* in their classrooms and schools, and they can take steps to investigate many difficulties and construct their own approaches to assisting children.

In addition to consulting with outside specialists, there are many advantages in consulting with teaching colleagues on the school staff. Unlike the classroom teacher, the colleague has not invested effort and emotions into the context and relationships, and consequently brings fresh insights to difficult situations. Teaching colleagues understand the school context very well, and they know a great deal about the school culture, the families and the community.

Teachers find that it is useful to consult with a peer because they can work collaboratively over an extended period of time that allows trust relationships to develop. Teachers find that researching with a peer allows them to talk through problems at a deep level and reflect together on information gained systematically. In addition, peers generally do not experience problems about inequalities of power, looking good or saving face and they can just get on with the job. However, at times, even peers need to respond with sensitivity to situations where a teacher has to re-consider practices or own their harmful judgements about a particular child.

Teachers may recognise the benefits of conducting research but those with little research experience can feel overwhelmed by the task. Teachers may think that research is not part of their job and that they lack time for additional commitments in their overcrowded work lives.

Finding time to research

How can teachers find time to add research to their ever-growing list of responsibilities? The way teachers find the time to conduct a study will depend on the research topic, but it is likely that it will require teachers to recast some of their ideas about their teaching role. The *only* way that teachers will make time for research is to view it as an integral part of their teaching work, rather than an add-on.

There is a common belief held by the teaching profession that teachers are not working unless they are involved directly with children. The belief that teachers need to be interacting, organising or directly teaching children makes it difficult for teachers to take time out and stand back from the class to gather data on children and contexts.

The idea that teachers must always be interacting in some way with children is outdated, and originates in traditional teaching pedagogy. Constructivist approaches to teaching asks teachers to view children as self-motivated active learners who follow their own emergent interests at times, this can free up the teacher for research.

Allowing children to follow their own learning interests means being well organised so that teachers ensure that adequate supplies of materials and equipment are on hand, that children are familiar with classroom rules, and routines are established well. In addition, children's safety needs must be met. Reframing some periods in a week to allow children more autonomy may be one way to gain some time, this may not be more than ten minutes, but, regular blocks can add up to a substantial amount of data collection over a few weeks.

At times, teacher assistants can use a video camera or tape recorder, or they can be trained to make running records or use checklists of particular behaviours. Some teachers negotiate with the management team in their school to free up time for research in exchange for sharing their methods and findings with the staff. Other teachers use their preparation time, time spent on duties other than teaching time, to conduct their classroom research.

I suggest that the time invested in research will pay handsome dividends that will help teachers to save time in the future. Readers might like to think about how much time they spend dealing with uncompliant behaviour, and ask about the irritation, stress and negative feelings that are generated by managing the behaviour of one uncompliant child. Readers might like to reflect back to Chapter 4, and the case study of Tom who was diagnosed with ADHD. We can ask:

- How much time did Tom's teacher spend on him during a day and over a week?
- How much negative energy?
- How much stress did she incur?
- How much teaching and learning time was lost over the course of a week for all the children in the class? For Tom?

It seems reasonable to infer from the findings of the case study that the teacher spent a great deal of time and energy on Tom. There is little doubt that Tom's seemingly never ending uncompliant behaviour caused the teacher a great deal of annoyance. Time spent on research could have been a valuable investment for Tom's teacher. It is likely that she would have obtained some new information about Tom, such as insights into the relationships offered to Tom by the classroom context. The teacher may have been surprised to find that he complied with 65 per cent of her instructions, as it seemed that he was always *un*compliant. The teacher may not know that she tended to ignore Tom's compliant behaviour and pay a great deal of attention to him when he misbehaved. The teacher may have readjusted her cognitions about Tom in view of objective information about his relationships in the classroom.

In response to a teacher's plea, 'I'm so busy, how can I spend time on research?' I have to ask, 'How can you afford not to invest that time?' I think it is true that teachers will only spend time on research if they are convinced of its worth, which means having a good idea of the long-term gains from the research findings. It's a 'Catch-22' situation; teachers won't know how research can inform their practice unless they do it, but they won't do it unless they experience how it can inform their practice.

Engaging in research can be professionally enriching and empowering. Working collaboratively can break down the isolation experienced by many teachers and it can lead the way for change in the school context. The following section tells the story of one teacher, Liz, who experienced many doubts about her capacities to conduct classroom research but found that it was an exciting and invigorating experience.

The teacher-researcher

The beginning

Liz was a teacher who felt intimidated by the idea of conducting action research in her classroom. Liz reflected on her feelings, noting:

> I didn't know much about research ... I wasn't looking forward to it ... I wasn't a researcher, I was *just a teacher*. I just didn't think I could do it. I thought a researcher was someone who was a 'doctor' and knew how to do all this ... and I didn't think I was capable at all.

Liz talked about the mystique that surrounds research, which says something about the university academics who have perpetuated the myth. She thought research was all about, 'rats and stats', and she was relieved to know that she could conduct valid research without having to give the children standardised tests or make them take part in experiments.

Liz was motivated to investigate children's understanding of *design* in Technology and Enterprise, which was a topic that she found extremely interesting, however, she did not know how she could find the time to conduct the study. Liz was hesitant to plunge in and made many excuses to delay the start. However, she did eventually begin and gradually her perceptions of research changed.

Putting plans into action

Liz began to appreciate that she was in a privileged position as a classroom teacher, and she realised that she had specialised knowledge that was not available to 'outside experts'. Liz said that outsiders may not get the 'correct view', because they did not know the children and she observed that she was able to see the picture 'behind the picture', because of her insider knowledge. Liz appreciated knowing the history of her group of children, and she matched her expectations of the children with the school's culture.

Liz expected that she would need a great deal of help to understand research techniques. She did need guidance at certain points in her project, however, it was soon obvious that what she really needed was someone to listen to her plans and support her when she asked 'Is this right? Is this research?'

The study lasted a term, and as it progressed Liz discovered that her new understanding of research was informing many aspects of her practice. She realised that she was applying her research knowledge to her daily classroom experiences by:

> Analysing what's happening, informing the teaching and finding out a bit more.

As the findings emerged

Liz's knowledge and confidence grew as she saw the results of the study. By the end of the study, Liz was no longer afraid of research and had developed a much more realistic view of it. She said:

> I know that *any* teacher can be a researcher, and that it's really valuable.

Liz's experience had eroded her previous awe of research that she'd read about in academic journals, and she started to take a much more analytical view of studies. As she talked she realised that her perspectives had changed and she said:

> I'm a bit sceptical about some research now. Especially the type where someone from the outside comes in ... far more valuable for a teacher to do it herself.

Before becoming a researcher Liz tended to accept the views of other professionals who were observing children in her class. However, since developing research skills Liz found herself being critically aware of the limitations of another person's view and she understood that different perspectives give rise to different knowledge. What became known and accepted as the truth was no longer a black and white matter for Liz:

> I'm very aware now of other people's observations, and um ... I'm quite sceptical. Just quite unbelieving. And I'm feeling that I'm looking in people's minds now and looking, trying to look at what they're looking at and saying, 'What are you seeing?'

As a result of conducting research Liz knew that research was a practical tool that exemplary teachers can use to investigate their classrooms, and she was more discerning about accepting other people's views without question. Liz found that she could not switch off from her newly acquired knowledge and skills, and although she had investigated the topic of concern to her satisfaction, she commented that:

> Turning off the project is the hard part! It doesn't stop! It's increased my awareness. I'm seeing more of these things that perhaps I would never have seen ...

Liz found that the process of research was exciting and satisfying. She found that the children's parents were very interested in the outcomes of her study, and she used the research findings as evidence to support her accountability as a teacher. Liz showed that she had changed her self-perception from being 'just a teacher', to a teacher-researcher, particularly when she described the study she had completed as:

> 'Professional research' and I think that says something for the school. Obviously the school has been supporting me and the parents have been supporting me, and that lifts the standard of the school.

Liz found that teachers are capable of conducting scientific research when they have knowledge of the techniques they can use and are motivated to use them. Liz was surprised at how much the research skills helped her everyday teaching life and she delighted in her growth of competence.

Collaborative research

Like Liz, many teachers are hesitant to embrace research because they cannot imagine how they could fit research into their busy professional lives. In addition, some teachers believe that it is not part of their role to investigate children's behaviour or classroom practice at a systematic level. Teachers who do accept the role of teacher-researcher change the knowledge that directs their practice. Exemplary teachers acknowledge that intuitive craft knowledge is an important part of their work, but they realise that objective data can inform their decisions.

Collaborative teacher-researchers can clarify aspects of school life that is shaping children's behaviour. School-based research conducted by teachers may engender a high degree of openness by the participants. Colleagues are likely to trust a researcher who has first-hand experience of the complexities of classroom life and a particular school. Nicklin-Dent and Hatton (1996, p. 47) said that the teachers in a study emphasised that they did not want to be scrutinised by a 'smarty-pants lecturer', but they felt differently about their peer researcher. The teachers thought their peer would understand their dilemmas and not judge them, and would understand why they used practices that were not sound educationally but were important to their survival in a challenging school context.

How can teachers make a start on research? Many teachers find that collaborating with other teacher-researchers helps them to tackle the new challenge of action research. Collaboration has many advantages, which includes helping staff to develop a shared language about their professional knowledge that they enact in practice. Talking deeply and seriously about teaching can lead to fresh insights into matters of concern.

It is important to acknowledge the difficulties that collaborative research can present, which includes the following points:

> First, isolation is a roadblock to collaboration. Isolation occurs when schools emphasise individualism and fragmentation rather than collaborative practice, and it may take insightful leadership to change the school culture.
>
> Second, teachers may be reluctant to expose themselves to possible criticism because it would result in loss of self-esteem. It is hard for teachers to invite outside observers into their rooms if they perceive them as 'evaluators' and fears about being criticised or evaluated act as roadblocks that stop teachers monitoring their own practice.
>
> Third, collaborative practice may be seen as a response to a crisis situation rather than being part of what teachers do to improve their practice as life-long learners.
>
> (Elliott, 1991)

What does collaborative classroom-based action research look like? I will illustrate it by recounting the experiences of one teacher, Anna, who had a great deal of difficulty with a small group of boys in her class. Anna kept a journal describing her problems with the children and she wrote:

> 1 March: Simon and his friends (Elliott and Christian) have been squeezing James out of their friendship circle: moving away from him

when he sits near them, not allowing him to play etc. James looks very confused and upset, he and Simon have been playing well together until now – how can I help?

Today's mat session didn't work well at all. I found it difficult to settle the children enough so that they were able to listen to the music, consequently they were unable to hear the sounds of the water ... Christian and Simon were disruptive, playing with blocks and toys from the shelves and pulling the puppet around ... I found myself nagging: 'Sit up', 'Face me', 'Listen'...

2 March: Elliott spent much of the time off task, rolling around on the floor. I should have been much firmer with him from the beginning, I probably gave him too many chances.

14 March: Several of the boys (Elliott, Christian and Simon) have been harassing the girls: setting up traps for them, running through their games and wrecking cubbies etc. The behaviour concerns me but I am uncertain how to handle it. Elliott also often kisses the girls or touches them during mat times. I realise that this behaviour cannot be tolerated, but where do you begin to tackle this problem?

15 March: Today's mat session was awful. James began by refusing to come to the mat. When he did eventually condescend to join the rest of the group, he sat well away from everyone else with his back to me. Christian wriggled around the edges of the group at times making strange repetitive noises and lying down. I tried to remain positive, trying all the strategies that I could think of to keep them on task (praising those cooperating, giving reminders of mat rules ...). By the end of the session I felt that I had made very little progress. Even though I had planned several motivating sections in my lesson, I didn't seem to be able to keep all the children on track. I began to wonder about what I was trying to tell them, and what I was doing wrong.

By 22nd March, Anna noted that Elliott and Christian were behaving in a more cooperative manner, and responding more quickly to her instructions at group time. Her focus of concern switched to Simon and she wrote:

I have found it really difficult observing Simon. He flits from one activity to another so quickly that I find it difficult to keep up with what he is doing. I had hoped to try event sampling today to record just how many times he disrupted the other children. In order to be able to do this properly I would have to be doing 'nothing' else except that. I will have to remain content with anecdotal notes to record the actual incidents that I happen to see.

23 March: Simon has really outdone himself in his efforts to gain attention (and wound my confidence a little at the same time) ... he was horrible and just seemed to go from bad to worse. During the mat session

> I had the distinct feeling that he was manipulating me. He was last eating fruit and seemed pleased that, at last, he had managed to have me all to himself, when I realised this, I left him to finish his fruit on his own (it didn't take long once I moved away). Is this a reasonable conclusion, or am I reading too much into the situation?

Simon's poor behaviour escalated and was particularly challenging at group time. Anna felt she had no other strategies she could use with him and her confidence was falling as she was at a loss to know what to do. As Anna noted in her journal, she was having difficulty in finding time to make the observations that she thought were important and consequently she lacked documented evidence upon which to base any plans to help Simon.

At this point, Anna talked about Simon with Judith; a colleague she trusted and admired. In the course of the conversation Anna was able to pinpoint her main concern to group times and after some discussion Judith offered to conduct some observations of the sessions and give Anna some feedback.

Anna was pleased to accept Judith's offer of help and was glad that Judith talked about some problems she was experiencing with teaching her class mathematics. Anna enjoyed teaching maths and offered to reciprocate Judith's help by observing in her class during mathematics. Anna and Judith agreed upon some mutually convenient times when Judith would visit the room in order to make timed 'running records' to describe everything that she saw Simon doing during group times.

As agreed, Judith made written records of her observations using objective language to describe the sequence of events as she saw them occur. She made running records on three days, in ten-minute blocks, that described all of Simon's behaviour and interactions that she had observed during that time.

Judith was a bit wary when she began the observations because she was not convinced that she would observe anything that would help Anna. However, after the first session she was fascinated by what she was seeing and was certain that the observations were going to help Anna gain some fresh insights.

Anna and Judith analysed the running records and made frequency counts of the number of times Simon complied with Anna's instructions and the number of times he did not. In addition, they looked at the running records carefully to try and identify any patterns in the compliant or uncompliant behaviour. They identified the sequence of behaviour: Simon's action, Anna's responses or the other children's responses, then Simon's actions.

Anna was open and responsive to the findings that showed she tended to nag and warn Simon repeatedly about his inappropriate behaviour at group time, but that her reminders and warnings were ineffective. Anna was surprised to find that Simon followed 60 per cent of her instructions quickly, because it felt to her that he was *always uncompliant*. However, the findings showed that Simon's behaviour had disrupted teaching and learning often during the group times.

Anna resolved that she must take quicker and firmer action. She decided to implement a behavioural programme at group time to reward Simon's behaviour with stamps and stickers when he followed her instructions, and to give Simon one warning when he did not follow her instructions. If he was uncompliant her assistant was to remove him to a separate room for two minutes of 'time out'. Anna thought that Simon was capable of manipulating time out by going backwards and forwards many times during a group time. She decided that if Simon was removed more than twice in a group time he was to sit out for the remainder of the session.

Anna endeavoured to implement the behaviour programme, but she experienced many difficulties in maintaining it consistently. Follow-up observation sessions by Judith showed that Anna tended to overlook minor acts of uncompliance, and sought to give Simon chances by reminding him that he was earning stamps and stickers.

Talking over what was happening with Judith helped Anna realise that she felt sorry for Simon, as he was a child who experienced many difficult challenges in his home life. Anna considered him to be a neglected child, whose mother implied that he was a burden to her. Anna's feelings of pity were making it hard for her to change her mental representations (comprised of cognitions and feelings) about Simon, which she needed to do in order to take more consistent action.

Anna and Judith decided to videotape two group time sessions, so that Anna could get a better perspective about Simon's behaviour. Before the videotaping began, Anna shared with Judith that she was beginning to doubt her capacities as a teacher and that her confidence was at a low ebb. After watching the first video session she wrote:

> Having watched the video of this morning's lesson, I don't feel quite so bad about my effort. The video shows clearly the effect that Simon's behaviour has on the other children. I was really shocked by this – many of them appeared to be really quite intimidated by him. When he was removed from the lesson, the others moved forward closer to me and participated much more. It is obvious that something must be done about his inappropriate behaviour.

Anna changed her perspective of Simon's behaviour by analysing the video of Simon's interactions at group time and discussing some key elements with Judith. She realised that she was doing a good job overall, which helped affirm her professional competencies, this in turn freed her up to start thinking creatively. Anna saw that Simon's negative relationships were not beneficial to him or others. Anna had not been aware of the dynamics between Simon and his peers, and she became much more clear that she had to take decisive action in order to help him and the other children in the group. Anna thought that Simon was in danger of developing roles associated with bullying, and that she resolved to help him develop more appropriate behaviours. Anna reasoned that Simon was, 'desperate to have friends', but allowing him to intimidate others was never going to help him make friends.

By reflecting on matters that arose from the findings with her research colleague, Anna gained some insight into her implicit knowledge that shaped her mental representations of Simon. Anna's mental pictures of Simon as a 'poor little boy' were hampering her efforts to deal with his behaviour fairly and firmly, and to maintain the behavioural programme. Anna realised that deep inside her she felt extremely sorry for Simon, and it was her sympathy for him that led her to give him one more chance.

Knowing how the children responded to Simon helped Anna to take a much more assertive stance with him and maintain the behavioural programme. As a result of implementing a consistent behavioural programme at group time, Anna observed a quick improvement in Simon's group time behaviour and consequently she was more motivated to spend some close 1:1 time with him. For example, she made sure that she sat next to him and chatted to him when he was eating his snack, whether or not he had been excluded from the group previously. In other words, Anna did not make her relationship with Simon contingent on his level of compliance. Gradually, a more comfortable relationship developed between Anna and Simon, although there were still many other aspects of his behaviour that caused concern.

Another result of the findings, evident in the observations and video material, prompted Anna to make some changes to the classroom environment. After viewing the video she observed that the toys on the open shelves distracted some children. Previously Anna had thought that children should learn to ignore to distractions but she changed her mind. Evidence showed children's zones of proximal development varied; some were able to resist the temptation to fiddle with toys but others could not. She turned the shelves around so that their blank sides faced the group, and she made the space bigger; this enabled all children to sit comfortably without touching another child or distracting objects.

In addition to changing the physical environment, Anna decided to pay greater attention to keeping the group times short because she realised that it was beyond some children's developmental competencies to attend in a large group for more than ten minutes at a time. Also, she thought very carefully about the content of each session and decided to have more action and less teacher talk. Anna realised that often she extended an activity because she thought it was important for all children to have a turn. However, she now decided it was more important to end activities while the children were still enjoying them in order to foster a positive attitude to group time.

The collaborative work between Anna and her colleague included the use of research strategies aimed to collect objective information. First, making a running record that documented everything that the child did and said within a given time period. Second, using video material to describe and analyse the behaviour of the child, the teacher, the group and the setting. The findings were powerful because they:

- enabled Anna to stop blaming herself for her perceived failings and to start appreciating that she was using many appropriate strategies, and so her confidence grew;
- helped Anna to change her mental representation of Simon as a 'poor little boy' to one that took account of the relationships between Simon, his peers, teacher, and environment;
- allowed Anna to see the classroom group more clearly. She stopped thinking about Simon in terms of individual deficit and was able to pay more attention to the context of the classroom;
- helped Anna to think about the context in terms of how it was supporting children's zones of proximal development. Anna improved the opportunities to behave appropriately by making changes to the physical context and the format of group times.

It should not be assumed that working collaboratively led to magic changes, as Anna continued to find that aspects of Simon's behaviour were troubling. However, she gained some profound and long-lasting insights from the collaborative research project. These were evident when Anna watched the group time video again two months later and wrote:

> 11 May: As I sat watching it, it dawned on me how much confidence I had gained since that early mat session. I can clearly remember the feelings of self-doubt and helplessness that I had felt as I struggled to manage the behaviour of a few of the children so that the rest could benefit from the lesson. I feel that I now have a good rapport with the children and have developed a much wider variety of techniques for dealing with specific situations. I enjoy being with the children instead of being stressed about what I am trying to teach … I never thought that I could change so much; now I realise I will continue to change for quite a long time …

One reason why the collaborative process worked was that Anna showed that she was willing to reflect on her practice and try out some new approaches. The relationship between Anna and Judith was based on equity, and Anna did not regard Judith's observations as evaluating her teaching performance. In addition, Anna was prepared to tolerate loss of self-esteem that could result from Judith's observations. She asked many questions about the classroom, which demonstrated her keenness to reflect on important topics related to the children's behaviours that she found troublesome. Anna was able to monitor her classroom practice accurately and was flexible enough to change her ideas in the light of new information.

Anna's desire to improve her practice marks one difference between research conducted by practitioners and research conducted by academics. Academics often seek to advance knowledge in the field and do not have the goal of improving practice necessarily. The classroom-based action research enabled Anna to refine her practical judgements about concrete situations that were affecting her daily working life.

The action research helped Anna to acknowledge the daily realities of classroom life with its messy complexities (Elliott, 1991). Anna was helped to clarify her original mental representations of Simon that hampered her ability to implement a consistent behavioural programme. Anna was able to use the evidence provided through the research findings to inform her professional judgements and her practical wisdom to create a context that supported children's varying zones of proximal development.

Talking in depth with colleagues can lead to staff visiting classrooms in order to participate in collaborative research. Staff may work together to design research instruments such as checklists, questionnaires or interview schedules, and can help one another to implement them. Staff can work together to transcribe and analyse data in order to identify appropriate interventions, and carry out checks to assess the efficacy of the intervention.

Collaborative research can change staff dynamics as teachers become empowered to take charge of troublesome classroom behaviour and work together to transform classrooms into productive learning environments. Researching with colleagues is demanding work, which should be recognised by the power hierarchy in the school. School leaders can reinforce the importance of staff collaboration by organising staff members to have time during school hours to talk to one another in depth, to reflect, to plan and to share understandings by talking together as a whole staff group (Corrie, 1995).

Collaborative research allows staff to:

- identify problems and brainstorm solutions appropriate to a context;
- use their knowledge of a context to inform their decisions;
- design and implement collaborative research projects;
- assess and evaluate the efficacy of the intervention;
- reflect and re-think until goals have been achieved;
- share their findings with the staff group.

In addition, collaborative research provides opportunities for teachers to:

- learn by imitating the model of a teacher they admire;
- talk about what they know rather than what they might do, thus going beyond tips for teaching;
- become mentors for staff members with less experience or expertise;
  develop a climate of mutual trust and respect based on positive relationships.

Skills of action research

Teachers worry that they lack the skills that are necessary to conduct scientific research. However, classroom-based action research draws widely on a set of skills that many teachers learn in their teacher education courses. These include the observation techniques of observing and recording children's behaviour, interactions, initiations and responses to peers, adults, materials, learning tasks and the environment. It is less common for teachers to use commercial questionnaires or standardised tests that require statistical analysis, which people often assume is an integral part of research.

The following plan has been adapted from Elliott (1991, pp. 72–77), and I will use the example of Anna's action research study in order to illustrate how these steps might work in practice:

Step 1: Identify and clarify the general idea

The general idea is a situation that one wishes to change. In view of new information the general idea may change at any time in the research process.

> At the beginning of the school year a small group of boys exhibited uncompliant behaviour, but after six weeks of school most of the children settled down and began to cooperate and respond positively to instructions. However, Simon's behaviour was resistant to change and seemed to be worsening.

Step 2: Describe and explain the facts of the situation

Brainstorm your ideas about the situation and write down your hypotheses about it. Your hypotheses are simply your best guess to explain the situation.

> Simon's behaviour caused concern throughout the school day but was more troublesome at group time because he interrupted teaching and learning. At group time children were expected to listen, sit quietly and respond appropriately to the teacher's instructions. Simon disrupted by ignoring instructions or not responding appropriately, by interfering with other children (touching or 'hugging' them, playing with their clothes or shoes, hitting, pinching, kicking them, making noises or talking, or laughing in a high-pitched way at inappropriate times).
>
> He seemed to want to draw attention to himself: the teacher's attention and the children's attention. He seemed to want to be the 'King Pin', and appeared unhappy unless all eyes were on him.

Why would a young child behave in this way? The types of hypotheses we construct to account for Simon's behaviour probably tells us more about ourselves than Simon, for example teachers may reason:

1. Simon gained attention by inappropriate behaviour. He was ignored when he was compliant.
2. Simon had some personality problems and a difficult home life, and he had not learnt how to behave properly.
3. Simon was immature and could not cope with teacher-directed group time.
4. Simon was a social star who showed many leadership qualities. He needed guidance to make his competencies work for him and the group.

Step 3: Construct the general plan

Statement of idea

This is a general plan, which could have been revised as a result of steps one and two:

> Repeated observations will be conducted at group time in order to identify the sequence of group time events/actions concerning Simon that includes his interactions with the teacher and peer group.

Factors to investigate, change or modify

This is a statement about the factors that you are going to change or modify in order to improve the situation.

> In order to know more about Simon's behaviour the focus of research will be to gather more information about group times:
>
> - my instructions and Simon's responses;
> - peers' interactions with Simon, verbal and non-verbal;
> - the content and activities of group time;
> - the sequence of events surrounding Simon's behaviour;
> - the strategies used to reinforce and guide individuals' behaviour and the group's behaviour.

Negotiations

A statement about the negotiations you have had or will need to have in order to conduct the observations.

> Judith and I will agree the times that she will come in and observe group times in order to gather some documentary evidence.
>
> I will talk to Simon's mother about his difficulties and see if there are any unusual circumstances at home or if she has any knowledge that

> could be useful. I will tell his mother about our research plan and make sure that she is comfortable with the idea. I will ask her to give permission for our research plan by signing a letter.

Resources

A statement about the resources you need to conduct the investigation.

> Judith will be my main resource, although it is possible that I will need to borrow the school's video camera. I need videotapes.

Ethics

Researchers must consider confidentiality, negotiation and control. Information must be kept confidential until the researchers agree to release it. However, researchers must agree to whom the information will be released, and they must consider whether the information could be misused to harm another person (Elliott, 1991).

In Simon's case, information could be misused to establish Anna's incompetence as a teacher. Or children's parents may respond badly to information about their child's inappropriate behaviour, which could put the child at risk. In some cases, permission will need to be granted for children to be involved in research.

> I will obtain permission to film Simon from his mother. Judith and I will maintain confidentiality by not revealing the findings to other people, unless we both agree that Simon's mother should be told. Judith has agreed not to speak about the research project in any detail to other staff members. If, at the end of the study, we both agree then we may share our work with the staff.

Step 4: Developing the next action steps

This section describes the course of action outlined in the general plan in more specific ways. Researchers decide how the research should proceed, and how its effects will be monitored:

1. The analysis of information gathered in the general plan showed that:

   1 I paid more attention to Simon when he was uncompliant than when he was compliant. More attention was paid to Simon than any other child;

   2 Simon disrupted teaching and learning for approximately 30 per cent of group time;

3 Simon complied with 60 per cent of my instructions. Disruptions tended to be long and drawn out and once a negative cycle was started Simon increased his troublesome behaviour in front of the group;
4 I tend to give less assertive messages with Simon than other children. I tend to be slow to repeat instructions and at times my instructions are a little vague.

Action: I will draw up a behavioural plan for Simon that includes the use of positive reinforcers (stickers and stamps) for following my instructions straight away, and time-out for not complying with my instructions to:

1 sit down
2 keep hands and feet to self
3 raise hand to speak.

Plans for time out will be followed carefully: acting on my signal, the classroom assistant will come to the group, collect Simon and take him to the 'time-out chair' in the kitchen (out of sight and earshot) for two minutes (using a timer), when the timer rings he will return to the group. Two sets of time-out only will be allowed in any one group session, after that he will complete two minutes of time-out, then stay in the kitchen, sitting on a chair at the table with two books to read. The assistant will stay in the room, but busy herself with jobs. I will explain the procedure carefully to Simon and check that he understands the consequences and rewards for particular behaviour.

Monitoring effectiveness: My assistant will record all incidences of time out on a sheet for each day, and all stickers/stamps used as rewards will be recorded there. I will tape record group times for a week in order to monitor how I implement the behaviour programme.

2. The physical setting increased Simon's difficulty in complying with group time rules. He gets distracted by toys on the shelves and by other children crowded into a tight space.

Action: I will enlarge the group time space and move the shelves around so that their blank sides face the children and offer no distractions.

Monitoring effectiveness: I shall use the audiotapes of group times to monitor the effectiveness of the changes.

3. The sessions were much longer than I had realised, and included much more teacher talk than I think is appropriate for the children's development.

Simon seemed to find the activities hard and his behaviour quickly deteriorated if I spoke for longer than two minutes.

> *Action:* I will shorten the length of the sessions and keep strictly to twenty minutes. I will include more games, concrete experiences and child-focused activities and keep teacher talk to a minimum.
>
> *Monitor effectiveness:* I will use the audiotapes of group times to monitor how long I talked. I will check my programme plans to assess levels of teacher-directed activities.

Step 5: Implementing the next action steps

Plans for implementing the next step should be made in detail, and plans to monitor its effectiveness should be made and carried out.

> Results of the findings showed that Anna continued to experience difficulties with Simon's behaviour; this is when Anna and Judith decided that a video recording of group time would be useful. Evidence of the video recording enabled Anna to see that other children were threatened by Simon's behaviour, and in talking over her thoughts and feelings, Anna was able to clarify her image of Simon as a 'poor little boy'. The research evidence helped Anna recast her mental representation of Simon, which led her to implement the behavioural programme consistently. Simon's level of compliance rose quickly and many of his annoying behaviours became incompatible and faded. At the same time, Anna sought out many informal opportunities to build a respectful relationship with Simon and was rewarded, at times, with a shy smile from him.

As these steps show, the research plan evolves over time, and the steps depend on the findings of the previous steps. At times the researchers decided that they needed more information before proceeding to implement a strategy, and a step needed to be repeated or changed slightly. It is important to remember that no two days are alike in classrooms and teachers must always deal with the unexpected that can change or delay their research.

Classroom-based action research is no less ambiguous than any other element of practice. Like all teaching decisions, research is ethically charged and involves moral imperatives. The teacher has to decide which is the most appropriate method to use and whether to continue or change strategies. It might irk a teacher to reward a child whose behaviour has caused her so many problems. The teacher might think, 'Why should a child like Simon get the treats when the children who have done all the right things get nothing?' The teacher may feel that Simon should be punished but knows that previous attempts to punish have not reduced his troublesome behaviour.

The teacher must work through these issues otherwise they are likely to get in the way of successful outcomes for the class.

The chapter continues by outlining some common research methods that classroom teachers use to conduct research studies.

Research techniques

Observation

Many of the techniques used in action research will be familiar to teachers and help the teacher to record observations of events or situations. There are several different techniques to use to make the observations as objective as possible, although what is seen and written about is *always* filtered through the observer's perceptual system.

When making observations it is important to keep to the following guidelines:

- position yourself in the least intrusive position possible without your view being obscured;
- be discreet and avoid drawing attention to the fact that you are observing a particular child;
- write down everything the child does as literally as possible. Include tone of voice, body movements and gestures;
- keep what you observe separate from your interpretation of the behaviour. The rule is: first observe, then interpret;
- do not use absolutes such as *never* or *always*, as your observations relate only to the events you are seeing. Your interpretations should reflect only your actual observations. If you think that a child did not initiate contact with another child, do not write: *never initiates contact* but describe what the child did exactly;
- do not use language that attempts to describe the child's internal states. For example, you may think a child seems *happy*, but ask yourself what makes you think he/she is *happy*? Smiling, laughing, and interacting with others are the behaviours that could lead you to think the child is happy, and these are the behaviour to describe;
- do not use labels that judge children's behaviour. For example, I may think that a child is *bossy* but this represents nothing more than my interpretations of certain actions and interactions. The trouble is that behaviour I describe as *bossy* can be viewed in many different ways and you may interpret the same behaviour as *showing leadership*. The rule is to describe the actual behaviour rather than make value judgements about it.

Running records

The observer decides when to observe a child, for example, during a particular time of the day or during a particular activity. The observer records everything that occurs within a particular time frame; this should be for no less than five minutes in any one observation period. Running records provide a rich description of a chunk of child's life or a situation. In addition, running records describe relationships and interactions that children have in the school day. Running records are time consuming and it is difficult to capture a group's process because there is so much going on and the observer is likely to miss important events.

It is useful to make up an A4 observation sheet to ensure that the observer keeps their actual *observation* of the child separate from their *interpretations* of the child's behaviour. Teachers will want to experiment with their own format, but Figure 6.1 can be used as a guide. It would be useful for teachers to have a good supply of these sheets available for the observer to use as convenient.

Anecdotal records

Teachers use anecdotal records to document any unexpected events that occur in the classroom or playground. For example, two children argue about the use of a rubber and suddenly one girl throws a chair at the second girl, swearing loudly. As soon as possible the teacher documents the sequence of events as clearly as she/he can remember. It is useful for teachers to have a stack of prepared anecdotal record forms to enable them to quickly and easily record the event. The forms could be similar to the running record form.

Audio and video recordings

There are several advantages and disadvantages in using audio and video recordings. The main disadvantage of video is that it is intrusive and children may change their behaviour because they are self-conscious, but this has become less of a problem with the popularity of home video. Video is least intrusive when it is set up in a fixed position and left to play; this works best when the participants are fairly static, such as during group time. The advantage of a camera operator is that they can control the camera to zoom in and out when necessary and capture scenes of interest.

Audio recording is less intrusive but the quality of sound may not be good, and it may be hard to identify who spoke and who did not. Transcribing audio and video recordings is extremely labour intensive, however, technological developments mean that computer programmes to transcribe audiotapes are improving all the time. One option is to listen and watch an entire tape and then select particular episodes to transcribe. Alternatively the following procedure can be used:

Date: .... Observer's name: ....

Child's name: ....

Context: ....

Time of observation: ....

Time	Observation	Interpretation

Figure 6.1 A format for recording observations in a running record.

1 watch/listen to the entire tape;
2 decide on particular behaviours/interactions that you want to monitor;
3 create a check list, for example, you may decide to assess a child's level of compliance: how many teacher instructions were given and how many times the child followed them;
4 watch/listen to the tape again and use the checklist to record levels of compliance;
5 watch/listen to the tape and transcribe several relevant examples of when the child did/did not follow instructions.

Keeping a checklist and transcribing several examples allows you to analyse *quantitative* and *qualitative* data. Quantitative data tells you how often the behaviour occurred, and qualitative data provides a detailed description of the behaviour.

Photographs

Many schools have digital cameras that are inexpensive to use and provide useful research evidence about the physical environment: pupil and teacher posture and body language, friendship groups, and the use of materials and equipment. A series of timed photographs can capture the sequence of events succinctly and be used as an accurate record.

Interviewing

Talking with classroom participants can provide the researcher with valuable insights into different perspectives. One strategy Anna could have used when investigating Simon's troublesome behaviour was to talk to him and other children about their understandings of the situation. One difficulty in interviewing children is that they may think they need to give the right answer or information that will please the teacher, but teachers who develop trust relationships with their children often overcome these barriers. Peer interviews can be very effective depending on the age and preparation of the children. All interviews can be recorded and even young children are able to operate a tape recorder with ease.

There are four main types of interviews:

- *Structured:* The interviewer works out each question in advance and asks only those questions.
- *Semi-structured*: The interviewer works out a set of questions, but depending on the responses, uses follow-up questions that are appropriate.
- *Unstructured*: The interviewer waits for the interviewee to raise topics or issues and then asks follow-up questions.
- *Stimulated recall*: A video, audio recording or photographs may be used to help the interviewees to talk about their reasons for behaving in a particular way. Questions are used to prompt the interviewee or clarify points.

Checklists, questionnaires, inventories

Checklists draw the researchers' attention to certain behaviours, interactions, or aspects of the environment, and they structure the information that is gathered. The limitation of a checklist is that rarely can it give the sequence of events or the detail of an interaction. It is recommended that they are used in conjunction with open techniques such as running records.

Questionnaires are a list of questions that help the researcher to quantify the percentage of people that think one way or another about an issue. For example, in Figure 6.2 the teacher wanted to know how many parents supported the homework policy and asked a series of questions.

Inventories give more information than a simple questionnaire as it consists of a list of statements and degrees of response. For example, a teacher may want to know whether the parents agreed about homework, and might construct an inventory that made statements such as:

Once the teacher has gathered information about the numbers of parents thinking one way or another about homework, it would be useful to interview some parents to gain some in-depth knowledge about their reasons for their views.

Nine year olds do not need homework (Please circle one)

strongly agree	agree	neither agree nor disagree	disagree	strongly disagree

Document analysis

Elliott (1991, p. 78) notes that documents can provide evidence relevant to the focus of research, these might include:

- curriculum documents;
- children's work samples;
- results of tests;
- assessment and evaluation of learning;
- communication with parents;
- reports of consultations with specialists and other professionals;
- reports to principal, staff and parents.

Professional journals

As Anna's story showed, she made regular entries in her professional journal that documented her personal observations, feelings, reactions, interpretations, reflections, hunches, hypotheses and explanations (Elliott, 1991). Anna asked herself questions in her journal and documented anecdotes of the children's behaviour and interactions. Anna's journal helped her to reconstruct her experience and it became a useful tool of research for Judith, as she was able to read her entries and use them as a basis for their discussions that monitored the effectiveness of their strategies.

All journal entries should be dated. It is useful for the teacher to write only on the right hand side of the page, which leaves the left-hand side of the page for later reflections and it leaves space for the collaborator to make comments,

Name: .... (Please tick one box in answer to each question)		
	Yes	No
Should nine year olds be set homework?	❑	❑
	Yes	No
Should homework be set every night?	❑	❑
How long should homework last:		
less than 30 minutes?	❑	
30 – 60 mintues?	❑	
more than 60 minutes	❑	
	Yes	No
Should parents work with the child?	❑	❑
	Yes	No
In general, are you satisfied with the homework policy?	❑	❑
	Yes	No
In general, does your child respond well to homework?	❑	❑
Please add any other comments you wish to make about the homework policy		

Figure 6.2 Homework questionnaire.

ask questions or reflect on their own experience. Collaborators must be sensitive in their approach to an individual's journal and their comments and questions should aim to deepen the teacher's process of monitoring and must not evaluate or judge the teacher's practice.

This section has outlined some research techniques that teachers can use in order to gather systematic data. In the following section a different approach to investigating classrooms is outlined.

The appreciative inquiry

The aim of the appreciative inquiry is to identify what works in classrooms in order to have more of it, which contrasts with the typical problem-solving approach (Hammond, 1998). It has been used most in the commercial sector, but educators such as Watkins and Wagner (2000, p. 42) have highlighted the need of this approach in education. The appreciative inquiry focuses on the positives rather than the problems. As I discussed in the previous section, classroom-based action research requires teachers to:

- acknowledge that they have a problem;
- identify a problem;
- diagnose the problem;
- look for solutions.

Action research assumes that teachers must look for what's wrong or broken and fix it; the aim is to have less of something that we don't do well. The focus on difficulties and what is wrong acts as a filter to reality and schools tend to see everything through that filter. Reality is shaped by mental representations, which are perceptions, cognitions, emotions, expectations and motivations. If teachers want to see how data conflicts with assumptions then they need to change the filter. However, this is hard to do because new information may be ignored if it doesn't fit the school's reality, and gradually tunnel vision develops.

The process of appreciative inquiry can help teachers to change the filter that constructs reality. Appreciative inquiry is based on a philosophy that is different from the problem-solving model because it helps teachers to identify the strengths of the context rather than the problems.

Appreciative inquiry asks teachers to:

- identify what works in their classroom by asking, 'What do we do well?'
- identify how they want the classroom to be;
- identify a time and situation when their strategies did work and the classroom felt 'right';
- create a dialogue to have more of those times and situations.

The aims of the change process are ground in real life experience. For example, applying appreciative inquiry to Anna, she would:

- *Think about what works*: Anna identified a couple of group times when all the children (including Simon) responded quickly to her instructions and were involved and interested in the topic.
- *Recall a specific time and event when it worked well*: She remembered that children were extremely responsive on one occasion when she brought in a live frog at group time; this had been done to reinforce several teaching points. Anna decided to stimulate a dialogue by talking to children after a successful group time about what they liked, for example, in the frog group time.
- *Work out how to have more of it*: Anna decided that she would incorporate more concrete experiences of high interest into group time teaching, and she would use self-monitoring to assess the strategy. Anna is motivated to try the strategy because she knows that it worked with the frog incident.

The reason that this strategy will be effective is easy to understand. It is not possible for children who are responsive and interested in the topic to be distracting other children, rolling around on the carpet, calling out or making noises because these behaviours are not compatible with responding to the teacher. When a teacher or class identifies what works well and decides to do more of it, then some of the problem behaviours are outgrown.

Steps in the appreciative inquiry process

The appreciative inquiry is a group process that a teacher can use in a classroom or a school can use with the staff group. Hammond (1998, p. 32) recommends the following steps:

1. Decide on the topic

It is important to spend time identifying the right topic for the inquiry because the topic will magnify a particular element of the classroom and it is important to magnify something that is worthwhile.

Let us take as an example the topic 'Working well together'.

2. Explore the topic

Asking questions is a good way to explore a topic. Teachers construct the questions when they want to conduct an inquiry with their classroom group. It is worth spending time thinking about the questions because the right questions will tap into something that is very important in the participants.

Working Well Together Appreciative Inquiry:

- Talk about a time when you thought the class was working well together.
- What was happening at that time?
- What were you doing and where were you when people worked well together?
- Describe a time when you felt proud to be a member of this class (or school). Why were you proud?
- What you like most about being a member of this class (or school)? Why?

3. Conduct the interview

There are many different ways that questions could be asked in the classroom, but depending on the age of the children, it would be a good idea for children to work in pairs and ask each other the questions. Audio recordings can be made of the discussion, or the children could talk about their responses during a whole group discussion and answers could be charted. Participants are encouraged to talk to each other about the answers to the questions, which may lead to more questions and answers.

It may be important to interview visiting teachers, teacher assistants and parents of the children depending on the topic.

4. Share the information

When the small groups or pairs of children have finished then the information should be shared with the larger group. The aim is to find out more about what the participants value and to uncover themes within the group. It is likely that participants will share important information and therefore their responses must be treated with respect. Regarding all contributions as valuable will lead to enhanced feelings of pride by group members.

5. Create provocative propositions

The provocative proposition helps to keep the best ideas at the participants' conscious level. The proposition comes out of the material recounted by the participants and it is based in reality because everybody knows they have experienced it once at least. In order to write the proposition it is useful to look down the themes that made the action possible. Children then think and talk about how this could happen everyday.

Teachers can:

- find the best examples that arise from the sharing;

- identify the circumstances that made the best possible;
- take the stories and envision what might be and write an affirmative statement that describes the idealised future as if it were happening, which is based on participants hopes for the future, dreams and aspirations that have been informed by their lived experience;
- write the proposition and apply 'what if' to the common themes;
- write affirmative present-tense statements that incorporate common themes.

Hammond's (1998, p. 42) checklist for provocative propositions includes:

1. Is it provocative? Does it stretch, challenge or innovate?
2. Is it grounded in examples?
3. Is it what we want? Will people (children and teachers) defend it or get passionate about it?
4. Is it stated in the affirmative, in bold terms and in present tense (as if it were already happening)?

An example of a provocative proposition for the 'working well together inquiry':

> In this classroom we respect each person's right to learn, to feel comfortable and to be valued as a group member. We build on children's competencies and interests by using learner-focused experiences. In this classroom we celebrate our achievements by sharing with parents, the principal, teaching staff and other professionals every day, and our classroom door is open to all.

6. Innovation and action

Hammond (1998, p. 52) emphasises that the power of the appreciative inquiry comes from the energy and excitement that is generated by the process. Provocative propositions help the group to remember the times when they experienced the best and it helps them to remember that they can achieve it.

A topic such as '*working well together*' could be applied to a single class, several classes that join together, the whole school, the children's parents and families, and to community members. It is suggested that participating in the process of an appreciative inquiry shifts in participants' mental representations from the focus on problems to visions that are empowering and positive. Participants will know and understand more about other people's views, dreams and hopes for the future, and much more will be shared by the group about their positive aspects, their talents, skills and knowledge.

Summary

This chapter has suggested some reasons why teachers might consider adding the role of teacher-researcher to their repertoire. It has outlined some strategies that teachers can use when undertaking research and some research methods. In addition, it has discussed another approach, the appreciative inquiry, which celebrates the strengths and competencies of a class, school or community rather than taking a problem solving orientation.

It is important to recognise that teachers are the experts in their own contexts. They have a wide range of skills and knowledge about teaching as well as in-depth insider knowledge of a particular school, class, group, individual children and their families. Teachers have the skill and expertise they need to gather and document data, and to monitor the process of changing children's troublesome behaviours. Working collaboratively can energise and strengthen the skills and knowledge that help teachers create harmonious learning environments in their classrooms.

Chapter 7

Investigating talking out of turn

In Chapter 6 I introduced you to some techniques of classroom-based action research and said that teacher-researchers don't have to use complex research skills that involve statistics and testing. Many teachers use familiar skills in their action research projects; this can include objective recording. This process involves designing an intervention and implementing it, and observing and recording to see if the intervention has made any difference.

Often teachers want to make a start in research but don't know where to begin. In order to help you identify a starting point for your own research, this chapter begins by presenting a research project that investigated a troublesome classroom behaviour that many teachers find difficult to manage: 'talking out of turn'. As you read the chapter, try and think about how you could apply the same principles to an aspect of classroom management or children's behaviour that concerns you, whether it is an issue of the whole group, small group or individuals.

The chapter makes some practical suggestions to help you reflect on your practice and make changes that may enable you to achieve your goals more easily. I aim to provide you with a model that you can adapt and apply to your context and troublesome classroom behaviours.

You may find it useful to think back to the material discussed in Chapter 3, which emphasised the importance of what teachers *know* and how it influences what they *do* in classrooms. As a teacher, you use management skills that fit with your knowledge about children's development, teaching and learning and the context of the school where you work. This is why it is important for you to investigate your own contexts and reflect on what you know about teaching and learning.

The teacher is only one part of the system and it is wise to investigate all the relevant aspects of the context when you decide to tackle troublesome classroom behaviour in a systematic way. It is just as appropriate for you to examine your management practices as it is for you to investigate and focus on the individual child. In the following section I report the 'talking out of turn' study, and use it as an example of how teachers can investigate their own classrooms.

Talking out of turn

Talking out of turn is a pervasive troublesome classroom behaviour that disrupts teaching and learning and causes a great deal of annoyance to teachers. Talking out of turn occurs when children ignore the turn-taking rules that operate in the context. Children talk out of turn when they talk at the same time as the teacher or their peers, interrupt another person's turn, or attempt to take another person's turn to speak.

The talking out of turn study was conducted in 11 schools in inner-London (Corrie, 1993). I observed and audio-recorded group times to see when talking out of turn occurred, how often it occurred and how teachers and students responded to it. Findings showed that talking out of turn happened in every classroom I visited but it varied. In some classrooms there was barely five seconds when nobody was talking out of turn but there was far less in other rooms. I investigated group time because most teachers agreed that managing talk at group time caused problems. Teachers reported that they had difficulty giving everybody a fair turn and not letting some children dominate the talk. Some teachers said that they found it difficult to maintain all the children's attention, and often children interrupted their teaching time by calling out, talking to others, or taking another persons' turn to speak.

Whole group story time was held at least once a day in the classrooms observed, and teachers used story time to:

- introduce learning activities;
- reinforce particular concepts;
- develop children's oral language skills;
- have a relaxing time when children were tired;
- calm children down after a stimulating event.

After I observed in the classroom, I talked to the teachers about what they knew about teaching and learning and their theories of children's behaviour and classroom management strategies, particularly during group time. I transcribed the tapes of the classroom and the interview, and analysed the material to see exactly what the teacher and students did at group time, and then I looked at what the teacher said about specific behaviours. For example:

- Did the teacher remind the children about turn-taking rules during the group time?
- What did the teacher say in the interview about rules to govern turn taking?

The findings showed clear links between what teachers know and do, although many teaching decisions were based on implicit knowledge. It would be easy to assume that teachers who had less talking out of turn had higher levels of skills in managing behaviour. However, the interviews showed that teachers managed their groups according to the knowledge they held about how children learn and how good teachers' teach. The teachers found talking out of turn a challenge because the behaviour occurred many times a day, every day of the school year. Teachers spent a great deal of time trying to control talking out of turn, which frustrated and irritated them. They said that they had to control talking out of turn otherwise teachers can't teach and students can't learn. Teachers commented that they felt stressed when they were not able to reach their goals because they spent so much time dealing with this seemingly trivial and annoying behaviour.

Who are the good teachers?

It is important to emphasise that I was not looking for good teachers. I maintain that there is no one right way to manage group time, and that the teachers with less talking out of turn cannot be judged to be better teachers. I made no attempt to identify good teaching because a great deal depended on the context and how the teacher defined the segment of teaching and learning that was occurring.

Teachers had different ways of defining the learning experiences that went on at group time. Consider the example of 'having a discussion' and how teachers might define the process of discussion at whole group time. It is easy to assume that everyone knows what 'a discussion' means and that it means the same for everyone, but this is not the case. For example, one teacher said she would have a discussion with the children about a book she was reading, and the following conversation was recorded:

Teacher: Who knows what marigolds ...
Child: [Talks at same time] marigolds.
Teacher: ... are? Put your hand up if you know what marigolds are. Tom?
Tom: A flower.
Teacher: It's a flower, do you know what colour it is? Jamie?
Jamie: Gold.
Child: Yellow.
Teacher: (To Jamie) Yes, like its name, a sort of goldy yellow. (pause) (to another child) Sit properly.
Children: Several voices begin to speak.
Teacher: Waiting to BEGIN!!

This teacher interpreted a discussion as a question and answer session when the teacher guided children to give the right answer. At the same time, she reminded children about the rules and had to manage talking out of turn. The teacher's strategies were different from other teachers who sought to follow up children's interests and encourage individuals to speak.

Some teachers believed that an informal approach helped children who were shy or hesitant to speak in a group, therefore they did not have rules to govern turn taking behaviour. However, there were many examples that showed that the children who got the turn to speak were those who spoke the loudest and longest, and frequently these children were the boys in the group. For example, in one story session, the teacher came to an exciting part of the story and said:

Teacher: ... something dreadful has happened, (pause) (several children talk to their neighbour/or the teacher).
Boy 1: Storm (said quietly).
Teacher: What do you think happened? (leans forward, looks at group – many children call out comments).
Boy 2: Run out of petrol! (said loudly).
Boy 1: Storm (said in a quiet voice. Others call out suggestions).
Teacher: Run out of petrol?
Boy 1: No, storm, storm (quiet voice).
Boy 3: Battery went flat (shouts out loudly).
Teacher: The battery went flat?
Boy 1: Storm (quiet voice).

> (During this episode many other children were calling out suggestions, and others were talking between themselves. The teacher responded to the children who caught her attention, usually by the loudness of their voices.)

In many cases, the quiet or shy children failed to get a turn to speak, and many did not attempt to bid for a turn. The teachers seemed not to hear the quieter children's contributions, possibly because the noise level was high. In these classes, often a small group of articulate and confident children dominated much of the talk. Some teachers commented that ensuring all children have a fair turn to speak was difficult, and one teacher said:

> Sometimes I think I should stop him from talking, but he is so keen, and is just bursting to talk – he can't help himself! Then I think, 'Oh I'll let him have his say, then may be he'll let other people talk', but somehow it doesn't work like that! (laughs wryly).

These teachers wanted to promote a positive classroom tone where children and their ideas were treated with respect. However, often the noise level meant that they had to stop the group to gain children's attention or protect the rights of a child to speak. The teachers had to chastise children frequently in order to maintain some sort of order without invoking rules.

Often there was a great deal of noise in these classrooms, with many children talking at the same time as the teacher; but it should be noted that these teachers did not intend to have a 'structured' approach to group time. There was noise because teachers wanted to encourage children to use oral language skills. There were examples that showed that what the teachers know and do are linked closely, but at times, it was difficult for them to achieve their purpose and the goals they identified for the children.

The classroom and interview material showed that teachers could be categorised in two different ways. Some teachers treated story time as a special context, where particular rules of interaction applied, and I described these teachers as using 'classroom talk' to manage their group. Other teachers treated story time as an opportunity to have conversations with children, and I described these teachers as using 'conversation talk' to manage their group.

Interestingly, the teachers did not know that they were using a different style of talk in different situations, and many had not thought through their strategies in an explicit or overt way. However, their tacit understandings of group time and children's behaviour led them to implement particular rules and teaching strategies so that they managed children's behaviour in a special way.

Teachers using classroom talk

The teachers who used classroom talk at whole class group time would not use the same techniques when they were interacting with children in a small group, and they did not use it in informal situations.

At group time these teachers:

- asked the group many questions about the lesson content: 'What type of car was Gumdrop?';
- gave frequent reminders about the correct way to answer questions: 'Remember, we need hands up for a turn to speak';
- had well-established rules for turn-taking that they made explicit: 'I won't ask Daryn because I never ask people who call out';
- directed many questions to individual students, which meant they called on the student by name: 'Who knows the name of the boy in the story, yes Maneesh?';
- responded to students' answers with feedback often: 'So you think his name is William? Mmm not quite right, have another think' or 'Yes, it's Wilhem';
- used praise to affirm individuals' behaviour: 'Excellent answer Paul, you've been listening';
- made more comments about students' behaviour: 'I'll ask Kate because she's got her hand up so beautifully', or 'When people interrupt me it just slows down the story and it's very annoying'.

The group of teachers who used classroom talk used management strategies that were different from the teachers who had a great deal of talking out of turn. The teachers with a great deal of talking out of turn talked to the group as if they were having a normal conversation with two or three children, and I described them as using conversation talk.

Teachers using conversation talk

These teachers:

- asked few questions. In normal conversations people soon get disconcerted if one person asks many questions and the other person does not. The teachers tended to make a comment and then waited to allow children to respond: '*The story is getting quite exciting now*' (paused);
- if they did ask a question, they tended to ask them to the whole group and wait for somebody to respond: '*I wonder who knows the name of the boy?*' (Scanned the group);
- when students responded to the teacher's question, the teacher tended not to comment on the answer, but showed acceptance with a head nod or smile, and continued on talking. In normal conversation it would be considered to be inappropriate for participants to evaluate the other person's response continually;
- seldom gave praise or feedback to individuals;
- seldom referred to turn-taking rules and only intervened to protect another student's turn to speak: '*Oh no, Tom, you just interrupted when Davina was talking*', however they only commented on being interrupted themselves when the noise level meant that nobody could hear anybody talk.

Remember that these teachers could not talk about the types of strategies that they used at group time, which means they did not deliberately decide to emphasise the group time rules or not to give praise. If teachers aren't using strategies deliberately, how can we explain the difference between the two groups of teachers?

Some people might assume that one group is more skilled than another, but another view is that the differences relate to teachers' theories of teaching. The 'classroom talk' teachers said that effective teachers:

- must lead children's learning;
- know where children need to be going in their learning;
- organise the classroom for learning;
- structure the learning for children;
- intervene to teach children appropriate behaviour;
- are responsible for children's learning;
- need to assess learning.

The theories that the classroom talk teachers constructed were different from the conversation talk teachers, who maintained that good teachers:

- follow the children's interests;
- step back and observe the children in order to plan further;
- don't push the children into learning until they are ready;
- don't impose learning on the children because there is no need;
- respond to children's needs in order to facilitate learning.

You may find that thinking about the two categories (classroom and conversation talk) helps you to work out some aspects of your own knowledge and practice – does one type of teacher sound more like you than the other?

Remember, I'm only talking about what teachers do at *whole group story time*. In what ways are your ideas about managing talk at group time similar and different from the teachers I've described?

Do you have different rules depending on the purpose of group time? For example, you may use different strategies for music or different strategies for the first group time of the day. If so, how do you let the children know that different rules apply?

How do you signal to the children, particularly the high-risk children, that they are expected to behave differently?

In order to show how the teachers' knowledge shaped their practice I will describe what two teachers know and do about talking out of turn. Victoria used classroom talk, and Dawn used conversation talk at group time.

Two teachers

Victoria used classroom talk at group time and her management strategies reflected her belief that teachers must guide the children by identifying where they need to go in their learning. When talking about the teacher's role, Victoria frequently referred to the process of learning as a journey, and said that the teacher had to *lead* the children on the learning path. Victoria said that teachers must give the children appropriate tasks and allow them to experiment and practice; when mastery was complete, the teacher taught the next skill and gave children the next task to practice.

Dawn used conversation talk at group time, which she managed as if she was having a conversation with two or three others. Many of the skills Dawn used reflected her belief that learning occurs when teachers stand back and observe children's progress. Dawn said that teachers should intervene only when the child needed help, but they should follow and respond to the child's interests. When talking about her knowledge of teaching and learning, Dawn used the metaphor of opening a gate, saying that learning was like trying to open a heavy gate. The child struggles, the teacher sees the struggle and gives the gate a push, the child goes through and the teacher follows.

Teachers often find it helpful to identify their personal metaphors for teaching and learning. For example, Victoria used the journey metaphor, and Dawn used the gate metaphor to talk about the ways teachers help children learn.

Identifying your personal metaphor helps you tease out some of your implicit knowledge about children and your expectations about their behaviour.

Individual or group?

Victoria often stressed the importance of the group and the teacher as an active leader of the group. She said the teacher must guide the children, intervene when necessary and determine children's learning goals. Victoria's emphasis on the group rather than individuals was seen at group time. She managed the settling down phase of story time by addressing comments to the group and reminding them about what they did last time:

Victoria: We all sat on the floor last time, didn't we? Do you remember (eye contact to children at the back of the group, then sweeps round).
Children: Yes (in unison).
Victoria: I thought you did (smiles at group. Children quiet, attentive). Well, we've got a new member today ...

Why does Victoria say, 'We all sat on the floor last time ...' when she sits on a chair?

How do you manage the settling down phase of a lesson?

What would you say or do at to settle children and gain their attention?

The group is emphasised by Victoria using the inclusive, '*We all* sat on the floor ...' although she was sitting on a chair, and she used the tag question, '... didn't we?' which encourages the listeners to agree with the question. Victoria then follows up with a question that evoked a unison response from the group, 'Do you remember?' In this way Victoria is helping children to recall her expectations of the group's behaviour. There was a new child in the group, and Victoria's strategy helped him to learn some of her expectations of the group.

By contrast, the importance of the individual was a theme that Dawn talked about often, and it was reflected in her practice. For example, at the beginning of story time Dawn tended to settle the group by addressing comments to individuals:

Dawn: Joseph, are you sitting nicely?
Children: (chatter, make comments).
Dawn: Shhshshsh ... Eva.
Children: (Chatter, some children watch Dawn).
Dawn: (Begins singing) Oh, my ears hang low ...
Child: Miss, Miss, he's pulling my hair!
Dawn: I hope not Shane. Sitting on your bottom Michael. On your bottom Dean ...

Dawn emphasised the importance of teachers getting to know the individual child and developing close relationships with them, in order to help children to learn.

Rules at group time

Dawn and Victoria had different rules and expectations about talking at group time. Victoria maintained that rules were essential in the classroom. She said that respect is shown to children by ensuring that routines were monitored and managed carefully, and routines depended on properly established rules that provided all children with opportunities to learn. Victoria's emphasis on rules was seen in practice when she said to the children:

Victoria: Right! Now I'm going to ask you a question, and I want you to put your hand up for it: What's the boy's name?

Victoria said that rule reminders helped children recall acceptable behaviours and gave them the opportunity to behave appropriately.

Victoria was seen shaping children's behaviour by ignoring a child who called out, and not selecting children who made noises to get her attention. She gave children reminders about the rules, and reinforced appropriate behaviours, for example, by selecting a compliant child for a special job. Victoria said that rules helped all children to participate and stopped certain children from dominating the talk or interrupting others.

Unlike Victoria, Dawn said she did not really have rules for speaking because 'the conversation gets so stilted when you do the hands up and wait till you're picked'. Dawn said that rules were not a priority and when it became impossible for her to understand or hear children, she just told them to stop, which is seen in the following excerpt:

Children: (Excited chatter, many children talking).
Dawn: Shshshsh.
Children: (Some quieten; many still chatter).
Dawn: Sohill, can you stop it now please.

Dawn said that the hands up rule was inadequate because often children shout out the correct response. She said that helping children reach the answer was more important than keeping the rule. Dawn said rules were unnecessary because children 'pick up' how to behave and they do not need rules to tell them. She said that children learn by imitating the model of other children, not by being told by the teacher. Dawn said that rules attempted to impose behaviour on children, but she preferred children to learn to take turns because they know it is acceptable to others, and it is part of 'natural' conversation.

What is your response to the teachers' opposing views about rules? Do you agree with either of the teachers, and if so, who? Think about how you *feel* about rules, and how you expect children to learn about and follow them.

The idea of 'rules' is a value-laden concept that taps deep into our personal experience, and clarifying how we respond to the notion can help us understand what we say and do around rules.

Do you feel uncomfortable about rules, or do you get a sense of security when you think about them?

Jot down the words or images that come into your head when you say the word, and give an example of when rules worked either for or against you.

The teachers' use of praise

Teachers who used classroom talk used more praise than the teachers using conversation talk. Victoria used praise to reinforce correct behaviour; for example, during the transition period at the end of story time she praised the child for correct behaviour and by allowing her to collect the toys. Victoria gave feedback to children about their achievements and their behaviour. She said that it was important for teachers to give clear messages to children because it helped them to learn academically, as well as learning how to behave appropriately. Victoria said it was important to use praise and encouragement because it succeeds in helping children behave.

Teachers like Dawn did not use praise frequently. Dawn said she wanted to provide natural learning experiences for children, which meant that she preferred not to praise. She said that she did not like to use praise to get children to behave in a particular way because it was false. Dawn said that teachers should only use praise when they genuinely wanted to recognise a child's achievement. Dawn thanked children when they complied, which reflected her belief that children behaved appropriately because they wanted to do so, and not because the teacher had imposed something on them.

> The two teachers offer very different views of praise.
>
> What is your position?
>
> How do you *feel* when you praise children for appropriate behaviour?
>
> What difference do you *think* that your praise makes to children, particularly the high-risk children?
>
> Begin to notice what you think and feel when you use praise in response to children's behaviour. Also, it may to useful for you to notice what you think and feel when people praise you.
>
> Notice how your thinking and feelings about praise shapes your use of it. Are you satisfied with your use of praise?

Asking questions

Answering teachers' questions is one way that children get a turn to speak at group time, however analysis showed that Dawn and Victoria used different strategies to give the turn to speak to a child. Teachers like Victoria asked questions regularly to mark the end of their turn to speak and the beginning of the child's turn to speak. Victoria often included the child's name, which she said enabled her to tailor questions to suit an individual child's learning needs.

Victoria maintained that the teacher must know children's academic abilities and developmental levels in order to ensure that the questions catered for the diversity of ability levels in the class. Victoria said that teachers must monitor children's changing abilities in order to help them move towards the learning goal. Victoria asked questions to scaffold learning, which is seen in the following excerpt:

Victoria: Let's have you Tet, Tet what do you think was the last thing, can you remember, the last thing that happened?
Tet: (speaks softly) The Iron Man ...
Victoria: Tet, Tet, say it again I can't hear.
Tet: The Iron Man ... and the farmer ... (inaudible).
Victoria: I'm amazed because you know Tet, Tet's remembered a great deal, well done. Right I can see you're bursting (to a child with hand up). Can you remember not to call out when someone's speaking. Put your hand down. Let's have Luba, what can you remember?

Luba: (speaks very softly).
Victoria: Say that again, say that again Luba.
Luba: (shakes head).
Victoria: No? You don't want to? What do you think Adiki?
Adiki: The Iron Man had disappeared.
Victoria: ... now I just wondered if anyone could remember some extra things that happened? You're all remembering bits of the story very well: let's come back to you Samuel, there's one more bit that I thought you might remember.
Samuel: When the fox run away.
Victoria: Who was left then? Who was left then?
Pupils: (Bid for turns with hands up).

Through the use of questioning, Victoria enabled the children to achieve the goal she set. Victoria matched questions to her estimation of children's capacities which fits with her knowledge that teachers should not wait until children are ready to learn, because she said, 'I expect to teach them'.

Teachers like Dawn asked few questions, and when she did ask a question tended to direct them to the group rather than to individuals:

Dawn: Here he is, here's Stanley – where was he then? (paused, scanned the group).

Often the child who got the turn to speak was the first child to answer the question, or if several children answered at once, the child who spoke the loudest and attracted Dawn's attention got the turn to speak. Dawn tended not to direct questions to individuals because she said it was important to wait until children expressed interest and then 'follow it up'. She said that she did not agree with teachers who, 'swamp' children with information and then expected them to, 'regurgitate it back' by responding to the teacher's questions.

Dawn often ended her turn with a comment and then paused, which allowed children to initiate comments or ask questions. The turn to speak was not directed at one child and often several children spoke at once, however this did not trouble Dawn as she maintained that it enabled her to follow up children's interests. Dawn liked children to have many opportunities to contribute to the conversation in their own way and to show their interest by raising their questions rather than always answering the teacher's questions.

The teachers in the study were not skill deficit. They used management skills that matched their knowledge of teaching and learning. All the teachers had well developed theories of teaching and learning that informed their decisions in the classroom. Many of the teachers in the study commented that they enjoyed talking about what they knew, and added that nobody had asked them to talk about these matters before.

Talking with others about what you know might help you to assess whether your aims are being achieved in the classroom. If your aims are not being achieved then clarifying what you know about teaching and learning might help you identify areas you wish to change.

Teachers like Victoria claimed to be encouraging children to discuss aspects of the story, but an analysis of the language of group time showed that children engaged in a teacher-directed question and answer session. Children answered the teacher's questions and did not have the opportunity to ask questions or raise their own comments for discussion. Victoria had less talking out of turn than Dawn, but children were not engaged in a discussion, which was the teacher's aim.

Teachers like Dawn often referred to social justice issues and wanted to give all children a fair turn to speak. They did not want to impose their ideas on children or expect children to answer questions without opportunities to ask their own questions or make their own comments. These teachers allowed pauses to occur in order to encourage the quiet children to speak. However, analysis showed that frequently it was the children who spoke the loudest or the longest who got the turns to speak, and often these children were the boys who attracted a great deal of the teacher's attention. Analysis showed that the quieter children rarely gained a turn to speak, and often the more confident children took their turn. In other words, at times the teachers' aims for social justice were not achieved.

The talking out of turn study showed that teachers knew a great deal about teaching and learning. Teachers appreciated the opportunity to talk about what they knew and how they provided learning opportunities for the children in their classrooms.

In the following section, the example of talking out of turn is used as a model to help teachers understand how they can go about investigating troublesome classroom behaviour. The process can be adapted to any behaviour in any context, and investigations can address broad concerns or a small and specific issue.

Making a difference to classroom management

Your endeavours to support appropriate classroom behaviour can begin by reflecting on what you know and how you enact your knowledge. Taking the example of talking out of turn, you can ask yourself about the routines and rituals that provide the structure of the school day, specifically:

- What is my purpose?
- What do I want the children (this child) to achieve?
- What is the best way to help the children (this child) achieve it?

It would be helpful for you to clarify their taken-for-granted assumptions about routine times, such as story time. Reflecting on the purpose of group time may help teachers structure routine times differently to meet their goals more effectively. It is not a question of teachers identifying what their purpose for group time *should* be, but what they think is the important function of group time for children in a particular context. For example, a teacher may think that the main purpose of group time is to:

- Develop oral language skills. If this is the goal, the teacher needs to ask, can this goal be achieved by having a discussion that involves at least 20 participants? Many adults find it hard to avoid interrupting others in a discussion with four or more participants, yet we expect children to manage this difficult situation.

  The teacher may decide that the goal can be achieved more easily by avoiding whole group discussions. However she/he may organise the children to form small collaborative groups. The small groups can work through tasks set by the teacher that are related to the story, and the results shared with the whole group. Small groups give all children an opportunity to participate orally, and roles can be assigned such as time-keeper, recorder and reporter, which may help to increase children's self-esteem.
- Develop group cohesion and self-esteem. If this is the goal, then the teacher may decide that simple guessing games, language games, or songs and musical activities may be more effective than a story.
- Relax children who are tired or over-stimulated. For example, after the lunch break or before home time. The teacher may decide to select a story and poems for children to listen to without expecting them to participate in memory recall or comprehension questions.

Teachers who identify their purpose and goals can check whether they are making accurate assumptions about what is happening during group time. The main purpose of group time varies, for example, one group time may be for children to 'show and tell' their news, and later in the morning it may be for story time. Different rules may apply at different types of group time. How can the teacher let the children know about the different rules that apply at different times? It is important to clarify the rules because the high-risk children may not be able to interpret covert or subtle cues.

Teachers can signal different purposes of group time by varying the physical seating arrangement. Show and tell may take place with children sitting in a large circle; story time may take place with children facing the teacher. Children learn quickly to associate seating arrangements with the purpose and the rules of group time; the teacher can give some children useful prompts if necessary.

Setting up a tape or video recorder to document some group time sessions will reveal interesting information to teachers, and may help them evaluate their practice. It may be even more fruitful for pairs of teachers to observe, make an audio or video recording, analyse the material and give feedback to their colleague.

Many questions can be explored with the use of good checklists and some audio/video recordings. For example, checking the balance of children who participate is an easy matter of ticking names of the class list. Usually a pattern emerges after monitoring three to five typical group times and often the information tells the teacher what he/she needs to do. For example, a teacher who is striving for gender equity may be shocked to learn that she frequently calls on boys to answer questions and thus excludes girls. This knowledge can help the teacher change her practice and ensure that she distributes questions more fairly, and further follow-up recordings of group times would help the teacher to check that the changes have been successful.

Readers should re-read the previous chapter to remind themselves about the steps recommended when interventions are to be implemented. In summary:

- obtain the base-line data, which is information about what happens normally;
- use the base-line data to plan the intervention;
- implement the intervention;
- check whether the intervention is working by recording and analysing the recordings with a checklist. If the intervention has not led to satisfactory outcomes behaviour, then begin the cycle again.

Investigating the context

There are many different types of questions teachers can investigate about group times, these include:

Managing Turns

1. Which children get a turn to speak in my classroom at group time?

- Do children talk out of turn? If so, which children and how often? Do some children talk out of turn consistently?
- Do they interrupt me and/or take other children's turns to speak?
- Do they tend to talk in a gap or silence?
- Is there a balance between girls and boys who speak at group time?

2. What strategies do I encourage children to use to get a turn to speak?

- give rule reminders (put up your hand to speak);

- give turns to children with their hand up;
- give turns to children not interrupting others;
- ignore call outs;
- respond when they talk in a gap or silence.

3. How do I allocate the turns?

- by naming individuals;
- by non-verbal means: pointing; smiling; head nodding?

4. Do children gain turns to speak themselves? If so, how? By:

- putting up their hands and waiting for me to allocate a turn;
- putting their hands up and making noises to attract my attention;
- talking in a space when nobody else is talking;
- talking more loudly than their peers and getting my attention;
- talking longer than others and getting my attention;
- interrupting others;
- calling out the right answer.

5. Do all children have opportunities to speak and participate?

- children learning English as a second language;
- children with special needs;
- children who tend to be quiet; who don't volunteer quickly.

6. What strategies do I use to encourage the quieter children to participate?

- pass around the 'talking stick'. The child holding the stick has a turn to speak;
- name the quieter children and given them a turn to speak;
- stop others from interrupting the quieter children.

7. Do I respond to cues from the quieter children that indicate they wish to speak? Cues might include:

- subtle change in body position;
- an intake of breath and prolonged eye contact;
- a hesitant hand-up.

Being aware of how turns taken or allocated at group time can help teachers to think through their values and expectations about turn taking, and information they collect can help them assess if they are satisfied with turn-taking processes. Objective information can help teachers to understand how turn taking might impact relationships. For example, if information shows that the children who talk the loudest and longest get the turns, the teacher might want to ask how this affects relationships with other children and the teacher.

Guiding behaviour

1. Does any particular child or group of children disrupt group time? What do I count as disruptive?:

- won't wait and won't put their hands up;
- takes others' turns to speak;
- talks over the top of me when I'm talking;
- makes jokes or irrelevant comments out loud or quietly to others;
- draws attention to themselves by misbehaving: sits incorrectly; touches others;
- refuses to follow my instructions or ignores my instructions;
- doesn't join in or participate properly.

2. If certain children 'dominate' the group, how do I feel about it?

- I like the lively children who are full of bright ideas;
- I resent the fact that some children insist on talking and won't stop.

3. If I want to change the children's behaviour, what needs to change?

- stop calling out: raise hands to speak;
- stop interfering with others: keep hands and feet to self;
- stop interrupting me: listen when I'm talking;
- stop taking others' turns to speak: quieter children must have a turn to speak.

4. Have I established clear rules that apply at group time?

- Am I sure what behaviour I expect from children?
- What are the rules and how have I established them?

5. If I have established rules, do I maintain them consistently?

- Do I tell children to put their hand up to answer, then find myself responding to a child who calls out?
- Am I sometimes more lenient and sometimes tougher?

6. How do children's relationships affect their group time behaviour?

- Where do children sit when given a free choice?
- Who do children chose as partners or peers in small groups?
- Are children mainly interested in getting my attention or other children's attention when they call out? How can I judge this?
- Are any children isolated from their peers, or rejected by the group? How can I tell?
- Does any child avoid contact with me? Do I avoid contact with any child?

7. Does the physical environment affect children's behaviour?

- Is there enough space and adequate light?
- Can children sit comfortably?
- Are children warm/cool enough?
- Are children distracted by stimuli that can be controlled?

8. At story time how often do I vary my presentation of the story? Do I use:

- large posters and pictures;
- interesting and appropriate stories;
- stories that encourage children's participation sometimes;
- big books, puppets, real objects;
- children's ideas as alternative endings;
- the children to dramatise the story;
- telling (rather than reading) stories?

9. If I want children to learn to take turns at group time, what is my plan for the children who find this difficult?

10. What is my plan for children who follow the rules?

Teachers who have clarified their own values and expectations can be much clearer about the rules they want to implement, and the strategies they will use when children break the rules. In addition to thinking about guiding individual's behaviour, it is necessary for teachers to think through the academic or curriculum content of group time.

The curriculum content

Clarifying the main purpose of group times will help teachers keep a clear focus and make the best use of the time. Including topics of interest to children in the group will serve to motivate children to participate in the group time activities. In addition, asking a variety of types of questions may encourage a range of children to participate.

1. What is my main purpose for group time in terms of children's content knowledge?

- How can I build on the diverse competencies of this group of learners?

2. Do I include topics of interest to the children in the group?

- How do I decide what interests the children? Do I ask them?
- Do I talk to children about what they are interested in and what they want to learn about?
- Do I listen to them and document their answers? Do I display their answers so that they can add to them or change them? Do I share their answers with parents?
- How do I plan to build on the children's strengths?

3. What types of questions do I ask?

- Percentage of closed and open questions?
- Questions that encourage children to make links between the content and their own experience?
- Questions that involve higher-order thinking skills, such as inferring and predicting? If so, do I allow thinking time?

Effective interventions

Collecting research data that describes the situation is only the beginning. Teacher-researchers will want to analyse and reflect on the information in order to plan effective interventions. In this section I use 'talking out of turn' as an example to show how teachers can work in children's zone of proximal development to plan and implement interventions.

The context

Teachers are in a good position to assess talking out of turn after they have conducted some structured observations that clarify group time dynamics. Research information can help teachers to evaluate how current behaviours shape relationships and children's opportunities to learn.

Teachers can ask 'What opportunities are helping these children to manage in the large group?' The opportunities include:

- relationships between children and adults; between peers;

- physical environment;
- rules that are established and maintained;
- curriculum content;
- length of time and seating organisation.

Analysing the interactions at group time may reveal that most of the children maintain turn-taking procedures well and that interruptions come from a small group of children. Analysis of the findings may enable teachers to identify particular group times when children kept the turn-taking process really well, and in accordance with the appreciative inquiry can ask, 'This is one group time that went well, what made the difference and how can we have more of it?' For example, teachers may find that when they change their teaching strategies or give more responsibility to children there are fewer disruptions.

Scaffolding children's learning of appropriate behaviour

Teachers scaffold children's learning when they help them to achieve something that they could not do without the teacher's assistance. Teachers scaffold by reducing the demands of a situation so that children experience success rather than failure (Faulkner, Littleton and Woodhead, 1998). Therefore, at group time a teacher may reduce the demands of the situation by shortening the length of the session, including activities to which the children respond particularly well, or to take half the group at a time.

Thinking about and analysing objective data (the research evidence) can help teachers to ask how they can scaffold the children's learning effectively and enable them to behave appropriately. For example, if a child experiences difficulties with turn taking, then the teacher can work within the child's zone of proximal development. This is different from either teaching children rules directly or standing back and waiting for them to learn by osmosis.

Some children, particularly those at high-risk of not achieving their potential at school, may find it difficult to behave appropriately without the teacher scaffolding competencies in the child's zone of proximal development. Children who are left to discover the rules of group time interaction may never manage it and may get caught up in a negative cycle of misbehaviour and punishment.

Teachers who accept that learning to behave appropriately involves children's and teachers' *cognitions* are more likely to scaffold behaviour. Readers will remember that previously I explained that cognitions include perceptions, expectations, memories, thoughts and feelings.

Children's zones of proximal development

Working in children's zones of proximal development means:

- identifying their competencies and their starting point. Identifying what behaviour can they manage without prompts, reminders, or cues;
- working out how to build on their existing competencies;
- trying out different ways to support their learning;
- working with their cognitions and helping them to develop accurate cognitions;
- providing support while they internalise new ways of behaving;
- stepping back when they have gained the required competency.

Identifying the child's zone of proximal development helps the teacher to plan how to scaffold children's learning. I will illustrate the principle of scaffolding with a story from my own teaching experience.

> Jayden was a bright, active seven year old who had been neglected as a baby, and was adopted as a young child because his birth mother could not care for him. Jayden's difficult first years of life were shown in his impulsive behaviour that made it hard for him to self-regulate or delay gratification.
>
> Jayden participated fully at group time, but he got into trouble constantly for calling out, taking others' turns to speak and interrupting me. I was quite despondent about Jayden's behaviour because it seemed entrenched despite my best efforts to help him learn to follow turn-taking rules. It seemed to me that Jayden had to be the centre of my attention every minute of group time and I felt overwhelmed by his demands. When I talked about my feelings with my colleagues I realised that I had been in a negative spiral about Jayden and I resolved to make a fresh start.
>
> One colleague volunteered to film three group times to capture an accurate record of Jayden's behaviour, and my assistant offered to keep a checklist of Jayden's group time behaviour to help us identify any patterns. Looking through the video tapes and checklists, I realised that I was wrong to think Jayden wasn't learning about turn taking because he did remember to put his hand up often but tended to call out at the same time.
>
> Working in Jayden's zone of proximal development helped me to acknowledge what he could do now and what he needed to do. Also, I realised what I needed to do, which was to help Jayden build on his existing skills and understand that the turn-taking process was:
>
> 1 Hand up;
> 2 Wait till called on to answer.
>
> I talked the problem over with Jayden. I showed him a segment of the videotape which helped him understand that he was getting some things right. I encouraged him to talk about how he felt when he wasn't called

on straight away. He said in a sad little voice, 'You don't see me. You might forget to ask me'. I was touched deeply by his honesty and ability to express his fear. We talked about how group time was different from small group time or 1:1 time, and I shared some of my feelings of frustration with him. Jayden was attentive and responsive and I felt better for clearing the air.

We decided that as soon as I saw his hand up I would send him a non-verbal signal (thumbs-up) to show him I had noticed him and to remind him to wait. Jayden responded quickly to the strategy and began to manage waiting for a turn, which meant I could reinforce his behaviour using rewards we planned together. In turn, I felt warmer and more positive towards Jayden, and group times became more relaxed. I didn't have to give the signal for long as Jayden internalised the behaviour and managed to use it most of the time.

Jayden's story helps to remind us that children's behaviour cannot be separated from relationships that have histories. Jayden's early experiences had led to his poor self-concept and fear of being forgotten, which meant that waiting for a turn was stressful for this high-risk child. However, I found Jayden's constant disruptions to group time annoying and had begun to feel negative towards this bright and eager learner.

Two important steps helped to change the negative situation:

1 I had to acknowledge my feelings, which helped me decide that I needed to take a new approach to Jayden's group time behaviour;
2 I had to talk to my colleagues honestly about my thoughts and feelings as I confronted difficulties in working with this child. Talking with others helped me to give voice to frustrations I was feelings and my colleagues' supportive and non-judgemental responses engendered feelings of trust and respect.

Teachers who are unhappy about children's progress, the classroom tone, or their own level of satisfaction can be helped when they become more analytical about their classrooms. Teachers find that reflecting on the knowledge they hold about good teaching can help them identify their purpose. However, professional development is most effective when it is a collaborative endeavour that involves giving and receiving feedback.

Objective evidence gathered through video tapes and observation check lists showed me that some of my teaching strategies were working. However, I needed to build on Jayden's competencies by working in his zone of proximal development until he had internalised the behaviour and enacted without support.

Talking with Jayden about the differences between group times and other times helped him to begin to change his cognitions, and his sharing about his fear of being forgotten helped me adjust my cognitions about him wanting all my attention. Jayden was hungry for attention but that related to his experience of neglect as a baby and toddler. I wasn't going to use his past experiences to excuse his current inappropriate behaviour, but my adjusted cognitions meant that I realised I must put scaffolding around Jason's behaviour as a priority in my busy teaching day. Jayden needed my help, and working in his zone of proximal development helped me to provide the scaffolding he required.

Summary

This chapter has taken the annoying classroom behaviour, 'talking out of turn', as an example to show how teachers can investigate troublesome behaviours in their classrooms. The research methods include those that are well known to teachers: developing checklists, observing, keeping accurate records, analysing the findings and reflecting on what you know in order to plan changes. These methods can be used to investigate different types of behaviours and can lead to fruitful change.

I hope this chapter will help to demystify classroom research. Yes, research takes time, but so does managing troublesome behaviours. Researching in the classroom can lead to fruitful action, which is far more satisfying that being on a treadmill.

Above all, classroom research is based on the view that troublesome behaviours emerge from the system that provides opportunities and constraints for children to behave in particular ways and therefore it is the system that is open to scrutiny, not the lone teacher or child. Classroom research can provide findings that lead to evidence-based practice, which means that teachers will be able to maintain children on positive developmental pathways and make tangible differences to their lives.

Chapter 8

Conclusion

Towards evidence-based practice

As this book comes to an end, I hope that you will consider that investigating children's behaviour in systematic ways could help you make lasting change in your classroom. Planning and implementing practice based on evidence may help teachers and children learn together in productive classroom communities. Schools that investigate their organisation and management can develop evidence-based practices to help children to manage well in all areas of school life. Teachers who base their practice on evidence have good opportunities to demonstrate high levels of professionalism that fit with new directions in education.

Ethics of evidence-based practice

Helping all children to succeed at school is part of the ethical imperative of the teaching profession. Teaching in ethical ways means that we create classrooms and schools that model social justice. Schools based on social justice are free from bias and unfair judgements, and give all children equal opportunities to learn. Schools have a professional responsibility to support all children to reach their potentials. It can never be ethical for teachers to turn their backs on a child or count off the days till the end of the school year when the troublesome behaviours become another teacher's concern.

Ethical teaching is much more likely to foster trust relationships in classrooms (Charles, 2000). Investigating troublesome behaviour is ethical because it enables teachers to gain different understandings of classroom and school life. Evidence enables teachers to understand the child better, which in turn can lead to changes in perceptions of the situation.

Teachers who gather objective information about children's behaviour find that the facts confront their subjective perceptions and interpretations. Watching a video of yourself interacting with children in the classroom may change your perceptions of the difficulties that you experience. Your views of children are likely to change when you talk to children about their understandings of who likes them and who doesn't, whether they think the classroom is fair, or if they feel able to do the work.

Relationships

The theme of relationships has run through this book. I have suggested that relationships are critical to children's ability to learn and behave appropriately in classrooms. Relationships with children extend to their parents and families, as the systems model helps us to understand how different elements within a system overlap and interact.

Behaviour in context

In the beginning of this book I said that I hoped it would help you to think about approaches that are right for the sort of teacher you are and the context where you work. Although I have suggested approaches and given some models, one of the most important things for you to remember is that behaviour is always situated in a context and that each classroom context is different.

When teachers accept that contexts are different, they understand that investigating the context is an important key to planning effective intervention strategies. The context includes many different elements including human resources, space, materials, equipment, organisation and time. At times, simple changes to school organisation or the timetable can have a positive impact on children's behaviour. At other times, difficulties require a structured and multi-faceted approach to promoting appropriate behaviour.

Examples in this book have shown that behaviour must be seen as part of relationships, context and academic learning. Put another way, relationships act as a zone of proximal development for children's achievement of their potentials. A child may be aggressive and rebellious, but the underlying issue may be identified as a difficulty in fitting into the group and struggling with academic work. The child's difficulty in fitting into the group is not seen as the child's problem alone. The child may require the support of a behavioural programme to help support appropriate ways of managing frustrations, but it is likely that the group needs to explore their ideas of friendship. The teacher may need to think through the subtle messages that the group receives about inclusion and exclusion, and also will need to plan to support the child's success in academic tasks.

Collaborating with parents

The systems model helps teachers to understand that parents and families must be provided with many different opportunities to be part of the school. Inviting parents into the life of the school is not an option but the professional responsibility of teachers and administrators.

Teachers can foster positive working relationships when they welcome parents into their rooms, treat parents with respect and seek to engage parents as partners in the child's learning journey. Parent collaboration is well developed in the schools of Reggio Emilia, where the educators stress that it is important to offer a diversity of activities to meet the various interests, needs and aspirations of different families (Spaggiari, 1994). Including parents' views in classroom and school research can lead to a great deal of information that can help to design effective change.

The practical difficulties in working with parents are recognised. Government policies that give financial support for this aspect of teachers' work are needed in many contexts (Siraj-Blatchford, 1994). However, there are many small steps that teachers can take to build positive relationships with parents that could make a difference to children's behaviour at school.

Collaborating with teaching colleagues

This book has explored the importance of collaboration between teaching colleagues. Teachers can reduce their isolation by opening their classroom doors to invite in teaching colleagues. Peer observation and discussion, sharing at deep levels, and talking about the meanings constructed by the staff can help foster trust relationships. Collaborating in research to investigate children's behaviour can lead to greater knowledge and understanding and enhanced professionalism.

Collaborating with teaching colleagues means avoiding the tunnel vision that can develop when one adult is alone in a room of thirty children for extended periods of time. It is healthy for teachers to be exposed to different ideas, views and perspectives. Debating, disagreeing and arguing a point can help clarify issues and point to a way forward.

Summary

I hope this book helps you move towards evidence-based practice in your classrooms and schools. School policy or teaching decisions should be based on information that has been gathered by investigating troublesome behaviours in objective and systematic ways. I hope you will find that the rewards you gain will give you confidence to adopt this approach when you need to find good solutions to problems that disrupt teaching and learning.

References

Addison Stone, C. (1998). What is missing in the metaphor of scaffolding? In D. Faulkner, K. Littleton and M. Woodhead (eds), *Learning relationships in the classroom*. London: Routledge.

Ainsworth, M.D., Blehar, M.C., Waters, E. and Wall, D. (1978). *Patterns to attachment: a psychological study of the strange situation.* Hillsdale, NJ: Erlbaum.

Asher, S.R. and Coie, J. (1990). *Peer rejection in childhood.* New York: Cambridge University Press.

Baker-Sennett, J., Matusov, E. and Rogoff, B. (1998). Sociocultural processes of creative planning in children's playcrafting. In D. Faulkner, K. Littleton and M. Woodhead (eds), *Learning relationships in the classroom*. London: Routledge.

Ball, S.J. (1987). *The micro-politics of the school.* London: Methuen.

Berger, K.S. and Thompson, R. (1996). *The developing person through childhood.* New York: Worth.

Birch, S. and Ladd, G. (1997). The teacher-child relationship and children's early school adjustment. *Journal of School Psychology*, 35, 61–79.

Bloom, L.A., Perlmutter, J. and Burrell, L. (1999). The general educator: applying constructivism to inclusive classrooms. *Intervention in School and Clinic*, 34(3), 132–136.

Bruer, J.T. (1998). Let's put brain science on the back burner. *NASSP Bulletin*, 82(598), 9–19.

Cassidy, J. (1999). The nature of the child's ties. In J. Cassidy and P.R. Shaver (eds), *Handbook of attachment: theory, research and clinical applications.* New York: The Guilford Press.

Cassidy, J. and Shaver, P.R. (eds). (1999). *Handbook of attachment: theory, research and clinical applications.* New York: The Guilford Press.

Charles, C.M. (2000). *The synergetic classroom: joyful teaching and gentle discipline.* New York: Longman.

Cole, P.G. and Chan, L. (1994). *Teaching principles and practice.* New York: Prentice Hall.

Corrie, L. (1993). *Pedagogical knowledge and classroom practice: teachers' management of a disruptive classroom behaviour, talking out of turn.* Unpublished PhD thesis, University of London, Institute of Education.

Corrie, L. (1995). The structure and culture of staff collaboration: managing meaning and opening doors. *Educational Review*, 47(1), 89–99.

Corrie, L. (1997). The interaction between teachers' knowledge and skills when managing a troublesome classroom behaviour. *Cambridge Journal of Education*, 27(1), 93–105.

Corrie, L. (1999). One size fits all? Early childhood teachers' responses to system-wide assessment reform. *Australian Research in Early Childhood Education*, 1, 32–45.

Corrie, L. (2000). Facilitating newly qualified teachers' growth as collaborative practitioners. *Asia-Pacific Journal of Teacher Education*, 28(2), 112–121.

Corrie, L. and Leitao, N. (1999). The development of well being: young children's knowledge of their support networks and social competence. *Australian Journal of Early Childhood*, 24(3), 25–32.

Corrie, L., Chadbourne, R. and Maloney, C. (1998). *Exemplifying and validating processional standards for highly accomplished early childhood teachers.* Unpublished research project. Perth, Western Australia: Edith Cowan University.

Crittenden, P.M. (1992). Quality of attachment in the preschool years. *Development and Psychopathology*, 4, 209–242.

Dodge, K.A. (1996). The legacy of Hobbs and Gray: research on the development and prevention of conduct problems. *Peabody Journal of Education*, 71(4), 86–98.

Dodge, K., Pettit, G. and Bates, J. (1994). Effects of maltreatment on the development of peer relations. *Development and Psychopathology*, 6, 43–57.

Edwards, C. (1993). Partner, nurturer and guide: the roles of the Reggio teacher in action. In C. Edwards, L. Gandini and G. Forman (eds), *The hundred languages of children: the Reggio Emilia approach to early childhood education*. Norwood, NJ: Ablex.

Elliott, J. (1991). *Action research for educational change.* Milton Keynes: Open University.

Elton Report (1989). *Discipline in schools.* London: DES HMSO.

Evans, T.D. (1996). Encouragement: the key to reforming classrooms. *Educational Leadership*, 54, 81–85.

Faulkner, D., Littleton, K. and Woodhead, M. (1998). *Learning relationships in the classroom.* London: Routledge.

Fields, B.A. (1986).The nature and incidence of classroom behaviour problems and their remediation through preventive management. *Behaviour Change*, 3(1), 53–57.

Fonagy, P., Target, M., Steele, M., Steele, H., Leigh, T., Levinson, A. and Kennedy, R. (1997). Crime and attachment: morality, disruptive behaviour, borderline personality, crime and their relationships to security of attachment. In L. Atkinson and K.S. Zucker (eds), *Attachment and psychopathology*. New York: Guildford.

Forman, E.A. and Cazden, C.B. (1988). Exploring Vygotskian perspectives in education: The cognitive value of peer interaction. In J.V. Wertsch (ed.), *Culture, Communication and Cognition: Vygotskian perspectives*. pp. 323–347. New York: Cambridge University Press.

Gauvain, M. (1998). Thinking in niches: sociocultural influences on cognitive development. In D. Faulkner, K. Littleton and M. Woodhead (eds), *Learning relationships in the classroom*. London: Routledge.

Gerovich, L. (1999). *The social construction of the child labelled as Attention-Deficit Hyperactivity Disordered.* Unpublished research project. Perth, Western Australia: Edith Cowan University.

Ginott, H.G. (1972). *Teacher and child.* New York: Macmillan.

Gordon, G. (1974). *Teacher effectiveness training.* New York: David McKay.

Green, J. and Weade, R. (1985). Reading between the words: social cues to lesson participation. *Theory Into Practice*, 24, 14–20.

Hail, J. (2000). Classroom concerns. *Teaching PreK–8*, 31(1), 88.

Hammond, L. (1998). *The thin book of appreciative inquiry.* London: BT press.

Hardin, C.J. and Harris, E.A. (2000). Managing classroom crises. *Phi Delta Kappa Fastbacks*, 465, 7–48.

Hayden, C. (1997). *Children excluded from primary school: debates, evidence, responses.* Buckingham: Open University.

Horsch, P., Chen, J.Q. and Nelson, D. (1999). Rules and rituals: tools for creating a respectful, caring learning community. *Phi Delta Kappan*, 81(3), 223–227.

Howes, C. (1997). Teacher sensitivity, children's attachment and play with peers. *Early Education and Development*, 8(1), 41–50.

Howes, C. and Hamilton, C.E. (1992). Children's relationships with caregivers: mothers and child care teachers. *Child Development*, 63(4), 859–866.

Howes, C., Hamilton, C.E. and Matheson, C.C. (1994). Children's relationships with peers: differential associations with aspects of the teacher–child relationship. *Child Development*, 65, 253–263.

Johns, B.H. (2000). Give peace a chance with research-based advice for teachers. *The Education Digest*, 65(9), 14–20.

Kavale, K. and Mattson, P.D. (1983). One jumped off the balance beam: meta-analysis of perceptual-motor training. *Journal of Learning Disabilities*, 16(3), 165–173.

Kohn, A. (1991). Caring kids: the role of the school. *Phi Delta Kappan,* March.

Kohn, A. (1993). *Punished by rewards: the trouble with gold stars, incentive plans, A's, praise and other bribes.* Boston: Houghton Mifflin.

Kounin, J. (1971). *Discipline and group management in classrooms.* (Revised edition, 1977). New York: Holt, Rinehart and Winston.

Kuzmic, J. (1993). A beginning teacher's search for meaning: teacher socialisation, organisational literacy, and empowerment. *Teaching and Teacher Education*, 10(1), 15–27.

Little, J.W. (1990). The persistence of privacy: autonomy and initiative in teachers' professional relations. *Teachers' College Record*, 86(1), 509–536.

MacNaughton, G. and Williams, G. (1998). *Techniques for teaching young children: choices in theory and practice.* South Melbourne: Addison Wesley Longman.

Malone, B.G., Bonitz, D.A. and Rickett, M.M. (1998). Teacher perceptions of disruptive behaviour: maintaining instructional focus. *Educational Horizons*, 76(4), 189–94.

Marlowe, B.A. and Page, M.L. (1998). *Creating and sustaining the constructivist classroom.* Thousand Oaks: Corwin.

McCaslin, M. and Good, T. (1992). Compliant cognition: the misalliance of management and instructional goals in current school reform. *Educational Researcher*, 21, 4–17.

McCaslin, M. and Good, T.L. (1998). Moving beyond management as sheer compliance: Helping students to develop goal coordination strategies. *Educational Horizons*, 76(4), 169–176.

Menter, I. (1995). What newly qualified teachers really need: evidence from a support group. *Teacher Development*, October, 15–21.

Moll, L.C. and Whitmore, K.F. (1998). Vygotsky in classroom practice: Moving from individual transmission to social transaction. In D. Faulkner, K. Littleton and M. Woodhead (eds), *Learning relationships in the classroom*. pp. 131–155. London: Routledge.

Moore, L. (1999). *Teachers' knowledge and practice when providing opportunities for children to develop as empowered learners.* Unpublished MA thesis. Perth, Western Australia: Edith Cowan University.

National Crime Prevention (1999). *Pathways to prevention: developmental and early intervention approaches to crime in Australia.* Barton, ACT: Commonwealth of Australia, Attorney-General's Department.

National Heath and Medical Research Council (1997). *Attention deficit hyperactivity disorder (ADHD).* Canberra, ACT: Commonwealth of Australia.

Nias, J. (1985). Reference groups in primary teaching. In S.J. Ball and I.F. Goodson (eds), *Teachers' lives and careers.* Lewes: Falmer.

Nicholls, D. and Houghton, S. (1995). The effect of Canter's assertive discipline program on teacher and student behaviour. *British Journal of Educational Psychology*, 65(2), 197–210.

Nicklin-Dent, J. and Hatton, E. (1996). Education and poverty: an Australian primary school case study. *Australian Journal of Education*, 40(1), 46–64.

Pianta, R.C. (1997). Adult–child relationship processes and early schooling. *Early education and Development*, 8, 11–26.

Pianta, R.C. (1999). *Enhancing relationships between children and teachers.* Washington, DC: American Psychological Association.

Pianta R.C. and Walsh, D.J. (1996). *High risk children in schools: constructing sustaining relationships.* New York: Routledge.

Reid, R., Maag, J., Vasa, S. and Wright, G. (1994). Who are the children with attention deficit hyperactivity disorder? a school-based survey. *Journal of Special Education*, 28(2), 117–137.

Sarup, M. (1982). *Education, state and crisis: a Marxist perspective.* London: Routledge and Kegan Paul.

Seligman, M. (1995). *The optimistic child.* Boston: Houghton Mifflin.

Silver, L.B. (1995). Controversial therapies. *Journal of Child Neurology*, 10(1), 96–100.

Siraj-Blatchford, I. (1994). *The early years: laying the foundations for racial equality.* Oakhill: Trentham Books.

Spaggiari, S. (1994). The community–teacher partnership in the governance of the schools. In C. Edwards, L. Gandini and G. Forman (eds), *The hundred languages of children: the Reggio Emilia approach to early childhood education.* Norwood, NJ: Ablex.

Stake, R. (1994). Case Studies. In N.K. Denzin and Y.S. Lincoln (eds), *Handbook of Qualitative Research.* Thousand Oaks: Sage.

Tharp, R. and Gallimore, R. (1998). A theory of teaching as assisted performance. In D. Faulkner, K. Littleton and M. Woodhead (eds), *Learning relationships in the classroom.* London: Routledge.

Tulley, M. and Chiu, L.H. (1998). Children's perceptions of the effectiveness of classroom discipline techniques. *Journal of Instructional Psychology*, 25(3), 189–197.

Turner, P.J. (1991). Relations between attachment, gender and behavior with peers in preschool. *Child Development*, 62, 1457–1488.

Vandenboncoeur, J.A. (1997). Child development and the purpose of education: a historical context of constructivism in teacher education. In V. Richardson (ed.), Constructivist teacher education: building new understandings. London: Falmer.

Van Acker, R. and Talbott, E. (1999). The school context and risk for aggression: implications for school-based prevention and intervention efforts. *Preventing School Failure*, 44(1), 12–20.

Vygotsky, L. [1934] 1986. *Thought and language*, trans. A. Kozulin. Cambridge, MA: MIT.

Watkins, C. and Wagner, P. (2000). *Improving school behaviour.* London: Paul Chapman.

Wertsch, J.V. and Tulviste, P. (1998). L. S. Vygotsky and contemporary developmental psychology. In D. Faulkner, K. Littleton and M. Woodhead (eds), *Learning relationships in the classroom.* London: Routledge.

Wheldall, K. and Merrett, F. (1988). Which classroom behaviours do primary school teachers say they find most troublesome? *Educational Review*, 40(1), 13–27.

Index